Words Mean Business

A Basic Japanese Business Glossary

by
MITSUBISHI CORPORATION

Times Books International
Singapore

Cover photography by Andrew Merewether at
Koharu Japanese Restaurant, Far East Plaza

Originally published in 1983 as
Japanese Business Glossary by
Toyo-Keizai-Shinposha on behalf of
Mitsubishi Corporation.

This authorised Times Books International
edition published 1984.

Editor: Rex Shelley

Editorial compilation and cover design
© Times Books International
  Times Centre
  1 New Industrial Road
  Singapore 1953

All rights reserved. No part of this publication may be reproduced, stored in a retrieval system, or transmitted, in any form or by any means, electronic, mechanical, photo-copying, recording or otherwise, without the prior permission of the copyright holder.

Printed by Singapore National Printers (Pte) Ltd

ISBN 9971 65 147 5

CONTENTS

Simplified Pronunciation Guide	8
Foreword	12

A BASIC INTRODUCTION TO JAPANESE SOCIETY

Hai and *ie*	18
Yoroshiku	20
Dōmo	22
Irasshai-mase	24
Tadaima	26
Okagesamade	28
Sumimasen	30
Shitsurei shimasu	32
-san	34
Kekkō desu	36
Zensho shimasu	38
Gokurō-sama, otsukare-sama	40
Chotto	40
Kao	42
Jin-myaku	46

GROUP ORIENTATION

Batsu	50
Senpai and *kōhai*	52
Dōsōsei	54
Ishin-denshin	56
Suri-awase	58
Uogokoro areba mizugokoro	60

INDIVIDUAL VERSUS THE GROUP

Rōnin	64
Gomasuri	66
Konjō	68
Kogai	70
Hiru-andon	72
Futokoro-gatana	74
Hijikake-isu	76
Kubi	78
Kuromaku	80
Ōgosho, insei	82
Newaza-shi	84
Tozama	84
Mai hōmu	86

FACETS OF JAPANESE SOCIAL AND BUSINESS FABRIC

Go-en	90
Hon·ne and tatemae	92
Gebahyō	94
Noren	94
Gaijin	96
Giri	100
Dame-oshi	102
Banzai	104
Abura wo uru	106
Apointo	108
Yakudoshi	110
Nippachi	110
Kaki-ire-doki	112
Goshūgi	114
Gashi-kōkan	116
Aisatsu-mawari	118
On	120

JAPANESE MANAGEMENT APPROACH

Kachō, kasei	**124**
Buchō	**124**
Kaigi	**126**
Nemawashi	**128**
Ringi	**130**
Negai, todoke	**132**
Soko wo nantoka	**134**
Hanko	**136**
Meishi	**138**

PERSONNEL MATTERS

Shūshin-koyō	**142**
Kibō-taishoku	**144**
Chōrei	**146**
Shaze, shakun	**146**
Seifuku	**148**
Jirei	**150**
Jinji-idō	**150**
Arubaito	**152**
Naishoku	**154**
Shukkō-shain	**156**
Teate	**158**
Tenbiki	**160**
Bōnasu	**160**
Shain-ryō	**164**
Kaki-kyūka	**164**
Yūkyū-kyūka	**166**
Seiri-kyūka	**168**
Teiki-saiyō, chūto-saiyō	**170**
Shin·nyu-shain	**172**
Aota-gai	**174**

INFORMAL CHANNELS OF COMMUNICATION

Ocha wo nomu	178
Chotto ippai	180
Aka-chōchin	182
Kangei-kai and sōbetsu-kai	184
Bōnen-kai and shin-nen-kai	186
Bureikō	188
Ohako	190
Shuntō	192

COMPLICATIONS OF LIFETIME EMPLOYMENT

Madogiwa-zoku	196
Teinen	198
Kata-tataki	200
Jihyō	202

THE JAPANESE CHARACTER OBSERVED

Hara	206
Hara-no-mushi	210
Hada	212
Shita, kuchi	214
Koshi	216
Ki	218
Te	222
Kara-oke	224
Kamikaze	226
Index	228

EDITOR'S NOTE

This glossary has been organised in a logical order, under headings which best contribute to a comprehension of the Japanese business world and its intricacies. It must be stressed, however, that words and expressions, adopted under one category, need not mean their exclusion from another. Overlapping into certain areas must be expected, but this order, we felt, was the most coherent one. Though *kao* can rightly appear in the final section, I have chosen to place it in the introductory section, it being a concept so fundamental to Japanese society.

SIMPLIFIED PRONUNCIATION GUIDE

In order to pronounce correctly the Japanese words listed in this book, all you need to do is learn the pronunciation of five vowels. The Japanese syllabary, which corresponds to the English alphabet, represents far fewer sounds than the letters of the alphabet. The syllabary contains only five vowels, 13 'semi-consonants' and one consonant – in all, seven less than the letters in the English language. (For the purposes of this simplified guide, we call the syllabary symbols which start with a consonant sound but end with a vowel sound 'semi-consonants'.)

The table below renders the Japanese syllabary in alphabetical letters. It also gives the diphthongs. The vowels and consonants are always pronounced in the same way without exception.

The constant pronunciations of the vowels are:

    a as in **a**nnounce   **e** as in p**e**n
    i as in **i**nk   **o** as in **o**il
    u as in p**u**t

The vowels which appear in the syllabary as part of the semi-consonants are always pronounced as shown above.

There are cases in which the vowel sound is prolonged. In such cases, in this book they are indicated with a mark above the vowel:

    ã, ĩ, ũ, ẽ, õ.

Simplified Pronunciation Guide

A guide for pronouncing the consonant sounds is not necessary because when, say, **k** is coupled with the constant sound of any of the five vowels, it can have only one possible sound. The only consonant that needs an explanation is **g**. This is always hard as in the English word **go**.

The diphthongs are combinations of some of the semi-consonants with the **y** line semi-consonants ending in **a** or **u** or **o**. In this case, the vowel sound of the prefixed semi-consonant is eliminated.

With one exception, all Japanese words expressed in the Roman alphabet end with a vowel. The exception is **n**. This is pronounced in a nasal way in much the same way as the English ... **ng**, but without sounding the **g**. This consonant comes only at the end of a syllable, and therefore in the words in this book, it is always followed by a semi-consonant: **banzai, hanko, denshin**, etc.

Sometimes, you will find double consonants in the middle of a word, such as **chotto** and **ippai**. In this case, the preceding vowel is pronounced with a slightly rising inflection and the first of the double consonants is choked.

When two vowels come together, pronounce each separately; do not run them together: **shain** = sha·in; **teate** = te·ate.

Simplified Pronunciation Guide

JAPANESE SYLLABARY EXPRESSED IN ALPHABETICAL LETTERS

Vowels   a   i   u   e   o

Semi-consonants

k line	ka	ki	ku	ke	ko
s line	sa	shi	su	se	so
t line	ta	chi	tsu	te	to
n line	na	ni	nu	ne	no
h line	ha	hi	fu	he	ho
m line	ma	mi	mu	me	mo
y line	ya	i	yu	e	yo
r line	ra	ri	ru	re	ro
w line	wa	i	u	e	wo
g line	ga	gi	gu	ge	go
z line	za	ji	zu	ze	zo
d line	da	ji	zu	de	do
b line	ba	bi	bu	be	bo
p line	pa	pi	pu	pe	po

Consonant

The one consonant is **n** which comes only at the end of a syllable (see above).

Diphthongs

kya	–	kyu	–	kyo
sha	–	shu	–	sho
cha	–	chu	–	cho
nya	–	nyu	–	nyo
hya	–	hyu	–	hyo
mya	–	myu	–	myo
rya	–	ryu	–	ryo
gya	–	gyu	–	gyo
ja	–	ju	–	jo
bya	–	byu	–	byo
pya	–	pyu	–	pyo

FOREWORD

Most people think of the Japanese as an enigma. That is because they are different. Not only are they different from the people of the Western civilizations of the American continents and Europe but also from Asians like the Indians, Indonesians and Malays. Even the Chinese from whom the Japanese have drawn many influences on language, religion and customs find them an enigma.

One important difference that many of us have to try to understand is their business style. This difference arises mainly out of their socio-cultural background, though historical factors of chance and economy have played some part in moulding the present Japanese business style. A general understanding of the socio-cultural background is therefore necessary before one can appreciate Japanese approaches to business.

There are a great many books available to acquaint us with the Japanese, the Japanese mind and their ways in the business world. They vary from deep descriptions of libidos and group psyches to straight crisp 'dos' and don'ts'. But all through these writings are references to Japanese words and phrases, because words embody concepts, and an analysis of their full meanings is a way of getting to the heart of particular thoughts and attitudes.

Foreword

In this book we have used words to give the reader a grasp of the Japanese business world. We have selected common and very significant words and phrases and explained their meanings and the nuances behind them. This is a quick way to sweep across the high points that distinguish the Japanese from Westerners and other Asians. In essence we have examined a series of concepts in detail which all together provides a background picture.

A résumé of culture and business methods would undoubtedly give one an overall background picture quickly, but such résumés carry many more generalisations and incur the danger of misinterpretation by the reader. A relatively disjointed collection of thought-pictures – such as this glossary – forces less generalisations but has the inherent disadvantage of not presenting an integrated view. It does, however, provide the reader who wants a quick introduction to the Japanese and their business ways, some points, pegs and milestones; and around these he can build more knowledge if he wants to.

This book was first originated by the Mitsubishi Corporation and published by Toyo-Keizai-Shinposha, to fulfil a need to brief foreigners quickly on the Japanese and reduce misunderstandings. They chose the glossary approach, but arranged the phrases

13

Foreword

alphabetically for easy reference. Unfortunately this original arrangement involved much cross-referencing and refocussing of attention. We have chosen to rearrange the same phrases in this edition under various categories so that the reader is first led through basic social attitudes and then brought into the business world.

In the first part, after a preliminary introduction to words and phrases basic to Japanese society, we show the powerful group consciousness that dominates the society and then reveal some of the subtler centrifugal forces of the individual struggling against this group dominance.

In dealing with Japanese business world phrases, we first bring in the more important methods which cut across all aspects of business before moving on to special areas of personnel, marketing, etc.

In the final section we turn to phrases that have particular Japanese meanings and illustrate both the societal and business thinking.

Some of the more specialised phrases which appeared in the first edition have been replaced with more commonly used ones. The Japanese translations (which were, incidentally, not word-for-word translations of the original English explanations) have been retained in every instance, though the English text

Foreword

has undergone some revision. The inclusion of the Japanese translations not only makes the book useful for serious students of the language, but it also meets a very important need: to show the Japanese themselves the key points of their differences with foreigners and thus makes the meeting of minds, over the negotiation tables, or in telexes across oceans, much smoother and easier.

We hope this book will contribute towards many a happy handshake, grinning and bowing after contracts are signed and sealed with the *hanko*.

Rex Shelley

Introductory words

The first words of this glossary are those which predominate everyday speech, but their translations into English nevertheless need to be accompanied by explanations or comments on their usage. For though they may include expressions as commonplace as *sumimasen*, meaning 'excuse me', they often contain nuances which may elude the foreigner. Dictionary translations do not convey the full subtleties of many Japanese words.

HAI and ĪE

Hai is 'yes', and *īe* is 'no'. *Hai* is one of the first words that you will hear. The literal translation is 'yes', but the usage and nuances are very different from the Western usage of 'yes', and reflect the Japanese character and style. In fact *hai* does not always mean 'yes'.

The Japanese would answer the question 'He does not speak Japanese, does he?' with *hai*. But it will mean 'He does not.'

The Japanese often carry over into English their peculiar usage of *hai* and *īe*, causing misunderstanding and confusion. Another problem that arises in connection with *īe* is that the Japanese tend to avoid using it. They do not want to embarrass or hurt the other party by refusing, denying or rejecting.

The safest thing for a foreign businessman to do is *not* to accept a 'yes' or 'no' as an answer but to persuade the other party to rephrase the reply in a sentence.

A misinterpretation that has occurred many times is when a foreigner describes a proposal to a team of Japanese businessmen. After he has completed his presentation, the Japanese bow and say '*hai*'. This *hai* does not mean 'yes'. It simply means 'We have understood.'

Hai and īe

はいといいえ

「はい」は yes,「いいえ」は no である。実に簡単明瞭なことなのだが,国際間のコミュニケーションにおいて,残念ながら日本語の「はい」は,かならずしも英語の yes の意味とはかぎらない。"He does not speak Japanese, does he ?" という質問に,日本人が「はい」と答えたら,英語の no と同じ意味である。その逆もまたいえる。

日本人は,その独特の「はい」と「いいえ」のつかい方を英語にもちこむので,誤解や混乱が起きる。もうひとつの問題は,日本人は no をつかうことをさけたがることである。断ったり,否定したり,拒否したりして,相手を困らせたり,傷つけたくない,という思いやりがあるからだ。

外国のビジネスマンが,日本人と相対するときは,ただ yes とか no だけの答えでわかったと思わず,yes または no のあとに続く文章も完全にいってもらうことである。これが誤解を防ぐもっとも安全な方法である。

YOROSHIKU

Yoroshiku is the word the Japanese often mutter during introductions, but the word is remarkably versatile. At introductions it means 'I am pleased to meet you', 'How do you do', etc., and carries the nuances of 'I hope you will be favourably disposed towards me', etc. When a person asks another to convey his best wishes to someone else, he says, 'Please say *yoroshiku* to Mr X.' When parting after a meeting or negotiations, Japanese businessmen more often say *yoroshiku* instead of *sayonara*.

The word can take on various meanings like: 'I hope you will take proper action'; 'Please give it your consideration'; 'I hope you will give us a favourable reply'; etc., without having to mention the matter in question.

よろしく

交渉や会議が終わって別れるとき、日本のビジネスマンは「さようなら」とはいわずに、よく「よろしく」という。初めて紹介されたとき、初対面のときも、日本人はお互いに「よろしく」という。だれかに best wishes を伝える (convey) ように頼むとき「どうかＸさんによろしくいってください」。

なににでもつかえることばだが、意味あいもいろいろある。最初にあげた例は次の意味である。"I'm depending on you."（あなたを頼りにしています）"I hope you will take proper action."（しかるべく措置してくださるものと思っています）"Please give it your consideration."（どうぞご配慮のほどを）"I hope you will give us a favorable reply."（色よい返事をお待ちしております）この表現は、問題になっている事柄を具体的に示さないのが普通である。

第２の用例では、"How do you do."（ごきげんいかが）とか "Pleased to meet you."（お会いできてうれしいです）と、つかい方は同じだが、"I hope you will be favorably disposed towards me"（よしなにお計らいくださいますように）というニュアンスがある。第３の用例では、"Give my best regards to ……" とか "Remember me to ……" の意味である。

DŌMO

Dōmo is another word used in many contexts. It means 'very', or 'much', or 'indeed'. In everyday conversation it prefaces words such as *arigatō* (thank you) and *sumimasen* (sorry). When it is unequivocally clear from the situation that you are either thanking a person or being sorry, the operative word is often dropped and only *dōmo* is used, instead of *dōmo-arigatō* or *dōmo-sumimasen*. When repeated in succession, *dōmo-dōmo*, it has the effect of expressing greater feeling or enthusiasm.

But the use of *dōmo* on its own is not as polite as the full expression *dōmo-arigatō*.

A salesman may introduce himself to a customer with a *dōmo*, have his order book signed and say *dōmo*, and leave with yet another *dōmo*.

どうも

「どうも」とは very, much とか indeed の意味で, なににでも使える日常語である。日常の会話で「どうもありがとう」(Thank you),「どうもすみません」(Sorry) といったように, ありがとう, すみません, などの前につける。前後の関係から, ありがとう, すみません, ようこそ, の意味だと明らかに分かるときには, 本体を省いて, ただ「どうも」とだけいうことがよくある。「どうもどうも」とつづけて繰り返すと, 強く感じている気持ちないし熱意をあらわす効果をもつ。

セールスマンが, まず「どうも」といってお客を訪問し, 注文書に署名をもらうと,「どうも」といい, 帰るとき, また「どうも」という。「どうも」だけですますのは,「どうもありがとう」などと, ちゃんと最後までいうのにくらべると, 多少礼儀にかけていることになるが。

Irasshai-mase

IRASSHAI-MASE

Strangers in Japan soon learn without being taught that *irasshai-mase* must mean 'welcome'. Because whenever they walk into a shop, a restaurant, a theatre, a bank, or even a friend's house, they are invariably greeted with this word. In fact, in some establishments it seems as if the only duty of the person stationed at the entrance is to bow and utter this word. If you browse through a department store, you will hear the word dozens of times because staff of each section greet the shopper with *irasshai-mase* as he or she enters their territory.

Banks and department stores train their staff in the correct manner of saying *irasshai-mase*: politely, deferentially, and with an affable smile. It is said in the same spirit as 'May I help you?' in English-speaking countries to put the customer at ease.

At places such as the fishmonger, greengrocer and *sushi* shops, which sell fresh food, the greeting is shortened to the spirited '*rasshai!*'

There is no standard response to *irasshai-mase*. A little bow acknowledging the greeting is probably the best tacit response.

Irasshai-mase

いらっしゃいませ

　友人知人の訪問をうけたときに歓迎して「いらっしゃい」「いらっしゃいませ」You are welcome, というが, 接客業ではこの言葉はとくに重視される。デパートや銀行ではできるだけ丁寧な態度で笑顔をみせながら挨拶するよう社員教育されている。

　内気で恥ずかしがり屋の多い日本人の場合, 用件もうまく切り出せないお客が多く, May I help you ? という意味で「いらっしゃいませ」といわれる。しかし新鮮さや意気を売りものにする寿司屋や魚屋, 八百屋の場合には, 「い」を省いて「らっしゃい」と景気よく叫ぶ。この場合は Walk up . という意味である。映画館やショーでも, お客を呼びこむのに必死になって叫ぶ。

　座敷で正座して三本指をついて「いらっしゃいませ」といわれるような料理屋だと, お勘定は相当に高くつくと覚悟しなければいけない。

Tadaima

TADAIMA

This word is often used, but it has two different applications.

First it is a word of greeting spoken by whoever returns to his home or office from outside. In a way it is an announcement: 'I'm back!' The full expression should be *'tadaima kaeri-mashita'* (I have just returned). Those within hearing would reply *'okaeri-nasai'* (Welcome back). Some companies require their staff to use these expressions as a matter of basic office etiquette.

The other way the word is used is in response to a request such as 'Come here!' or to do something. The *tadaima* in this case is like 'Coming, sir!' or 'At once!'

Tadaima is most commonly heard in small drinking establishments and restaurants. The customer sings out 'Another jug of beer, please!' The bartender or waitress responds with *'tadaima'* (Coming right up, sir!). But if it does not come soon the customer repeats his request. The answer this time may be *'Hai! tadaima. Tadaima.'*

ただいま

　直訳すれば just now にすぎないこの言葉を，日本人はかなり頻繁に使用する。

　まず，出先から会社や家庭に帰ったときの挨拶「ただいま帰りました」 Hello, here I am ! の略であって，これは出かける際の「行ってきます」 I'm going out に対応している。職場の出入りにこの挨拶をするようにしている会社もある。

　もう一つの「ただいま」は，人に呼ばれたり何かを頼まれたりしたとき，今すぐ実行するという挨拶の言葉である。たとえば小料理屋でビールを追加注文すると，「はい，ただいま」 coming right up, sir という女将の声がして，やがてビールとともに姿を現わすのがそれである。それでも仲々もってこないときなど，催促すると「はい，ただいま，ただいま」と重ねていうことがある。こんなときは却って遅くなると思っておいた方が良い。

Okagesamade

OKAGESAMADE

Okagesamade is an expression which reflects that politeness and consideration for others so deeply rooted in Japanese society. 'How is your child's injury?' '*Okagesamade*. He has recovered completely and is running around again.'

'How is business at your new branch store?' '*Okagesamade*. Our sales have been good from the opening day.'

Okagesamade is a word expressing gratitude and means 'Thanks to you . . .'

The dialogue quoted above could take place between friends and acquaintances. The people asking the questions are not the doctor or banker involved. The 'you' in the 'Thanks to you' refers to everybody in general, *including you*. The person who replies is saying, 'You also have a certain sort of relationship with me as a member of society, together with the doctor who treated my child and the banker who lent me the money to open my branch.'

Thus, if in answer to a question, the other person should say '*okagesamade*' (Things went well), or some appropriate response like 'That's wonderful'. If you should interpret this *okagesamade* as an expression of gratitude directed at you personally, and respond with 'Not at all', the conversation will take an embarrassing turn. (Or, perhaps, because you are a *gaijin*, it could very well lead to good-natured laughter.)

See GO-EN, GAIJIN

Okagesamade

おかげさまで

「お子さんのお怪我はどうですか？」「おかげさまですっかり良くなってトビはねてます」「新支店の業績はどうですか？」「おかげさまで開店早々から良く売れてます」

「おかげさまで」は字義どおりには「あなたのおかげで～がうまく運んだ」との感謝の言葉である。だが上記の例は，医者でも銀行家でもないただの知人・友人でしかない。とはいえ，なぜ「おかげさま」なのかと首をかしげることはない。ここで「あなた」は「あなたを含む世間一般」の意味であって，「あなた」自身も，治療した医者や融資した銀行家を含む社会の一員として縁があるからである。

したがって，なにかを問いかけて，相手が「おかげさまで～」といったなら「それは良かったですね」と答えれば良い。感謝されたのだからと「どういたしまして」などと答えたら会話はおかしくなる。もっとも「外人」だとかえってご愛嬌と笑い出すかもしれない。

→ご縁，外人

Sumimasen

SUMIMASEN

This is the equivalent of 'I'm sorry' or 'Excuse me'. Although the original sense of the word is an expression of apology for having done something wrong, it has several other common uses.

It can be used to call the attention of a person when you do not know his name. Addressing a waitress to place an order or addressing someone in the street to ask for directions is a typical use of *sumimasen*. It can also be used as an informal 'Thank you'. And it sometimes means 'Please' when asking someone for a favour.

The several meanings of *sumimasen* can surface during one situation. This is one instance. If you were to visit a Mr Hara at his office, you might say to the receptionist, '*Sumimasen* (Excuse me), I'd like to see Mr Hara. *Sumimasen* (Please), show me how to get to his office.' Upon meeting Mr Hara, you might say to him, '*Sumimasen* (Sorry), I kept you waiting', and as you leave his office, '*Sumimasen*. Sorry I disturbed you.'

See DŌMO, CHOTTO

Sumimasen

すみません

"I am sorry."とか"Excuse me."にひとしい。元来「すみません」とは、なにかまずいことをしたときに陳謝の意を表わすことばである。しかし別の意味によくつかう。

名前も知らぬ人に呼びかけるとき、ウエイトレスに注文するとき、道で方角を尋ねるときが「すみません」の典型的なつかい方である。形式ばらずに「感謝します」をいうのにもつかう。

なにかをして欲しいときには、どうぞ（please）の意味で「すみません」である。ある人を会社に訪ねる。受付で「すみません（Excuse me）、原さんにお会いしたいのですが」「すみません（please）、その部屋にはどう行ったらいいのですか」「すみません」（Thank you）といって原さんのところへゆく。「すみません（Sorry）、お待たせしてしまって」

→どうも、ちょっと

Shitsurei shimasu

SHITSUREI SHIMASU

Shitsurei shimasu is a very convenient expression for a foreign resident in Japan to learn. Its literal meaning is 'I have been rude' or 'I have lost my manners'. But the Japanese use it as a polite expression in situations and occasions when in English a person would say, 'Excuse me, but . . .'; 'By your leave . . .'; 'With your permission . . .'; 'With all due respect to you . . .'; 'Allow me to take the liberty . . .'; 'Sorry to interrupt you . . .'. Thus a visitor can use it as he is entering or leaving someone's office.

It is also used in an entirely different context to mean simply 'Goodbye' or 'Well, I must be going now'. In this second meaning, *shitsurei shimasu* is used far more often than *sayonara* in everyday situations by the person who is leaving. However, when you are saying goodbye at the airport upon your departure, *sayonara* is the right word to use.

You may initially find that it is difficult to decide when it is appropriate to use *sumimasen* or *shitsurei shimasu*, but bear in mind the literal translation of *shitsurei shimasu*: 'I am being rude' or 'I have been rude'. If you wish to be extremely polite and formal, you would use *shitsurei shimasu* rather than *sumimasen*.

See KEKKŌ DESU, DŌMO

Shitsurei shimasu

失礼します

「失礼します」は，日本にいる外国人が知っていて便利なことばである。礼を失しないいい方である。英語でいう次のような状況やばあいにつかう。"excuse me, but……", "by your leave……", "with your permission……", "with all due respect to you……", "allow me to take the liberty", "sorry to interrupt you……"

部屋などに入るときも「失礼します」という。逆に，「さようなら」(goodbye) とか「もう，おいとましなくちゃ」(well, I must be going now) といった意味でも使われる。このばあいに「失礼します」は，「さようなら」よりもひんぱんにつかわれる。外国のビジネスマンは，日本人を訪ねて辞去するときとか，パーティから帰るとき，「失礼します」といえばよい。しかし，空港で見送りにきてくれた人達に goodbye をいうなら「失礼します」でなく「さようなら」である。

→結構です，どうも

-san

-SAN

The Japanese don't have to worry whether they should address a person as Mrs or Miss. The suffix . . . *-san* is neuter gender and can be used for everybody. It can come after the family name, as in Tanaka-*san* or Smith-*san* or after the first name, as in Hanako-*san* or Mary-*san*, although Japanese men do not call each other by their first names. Sometimes, it can be inconvenient because upon meeting Tanaka-*san*, you suddenly discover it is a *she* and not a *he* as you had supposed.

The suffix *san* is also used with company names: Mitsubishi-*san*. A very special case is the mountain Fujiyama-*san*. A superior does not call his subordinates *san*. Nor do close friends address each other as *san*. The suffix they use is *kun*. Women friends, however, do not call each other *kun*.

In a business organisation, people with titles are addressed only by their titles, such as *buchō* (manager) or *shachō* (president). It is not only in the office that this form of address is used. At year-end parties and on the golf course, too, people are addressed by their titles. To the Westerner this may appear like a failure to draw the line between private and public life. But in Japan it is the accepted etiquette. In the old days it was considered impolite to call a person by name.

See BUREIKŌ

——さん

　日本人が女性に呼びかけるとき，Mrs.でいいのか，Missなのか，気を遣う必要はない。接尾語の「さん」は中性なので，だれにでも使えるからだ。姓のあとにつけて田中さんとかスミスさん，名のあとにつけて花子さん，メアリーさんとなる。ただし，日本の男性がお互いに名(first name)で呼び合うことは少ない。「——さん」は不便なこともある。田中さんと初めて顔を合わせて「あっ，女性だったのか，男とばかり思っていたのに」なんてこともある。

　接尾語の「さん」は会社名にもつける。「三菱さん」といった具合だ。上司はふつう部下を「さん」付けにしない。親しい友達同士も，だれだれさんとはいわない。このばあいの接尾辞は「君」である。ただ女性にはやはり「——さん」である。

　会社組織では，役職にある人には，その職名だけで呼ぶのがふつうだ。部長（manager）とか社長（President）といった風に，肩書きで相手を呼ぶのは会社内だけではない。忘年会などのパーティやゴルフ場などでも，すべて肩書きで呼ぶ。外国人には公私混同と思えるかもしれないが，会社以外でも肩書きで呼ぶことがむしろ札儀にかなったこととされている。これは，昔，人を名前で呼ぶことは失礼とされていた名残である。

　→無礼講

Kekkō desu

KEKKŌ DESU

You hear this phrase spoken very often at the dinner table. But watch out. It can mean 'This tastes good', or 'No thanks, I've had enough', or even 'That's a good idea, I'll have another helping'. Which of these three is meant depends on the speaker's intonation and on the linkage with other words.

Because of its many meanings, it is often used for repartee and jokes. The hostess asks, 'Won't you have some more?' The guest answers, *'Kekkō desu'*, meaning that he has had enough. The hostess shoots back with, 'If you think it's *kekkō* (meaning 'splendid'), you must have some more.'

Its usage, however, extends beyond the dinner table. In any situation, it can be used in its three meanings of 'good, fine, etc.', 'I've had enough', 'I'm satisfied', or 'with pleasure'.

Kekkō desu

結構です

　食事の席でよく耳にすることばである。しかし、要注意。その意味には「おいしい」もあれば「いや、いりません。十分に頂戴しました」もあれば、「はい、お代わりを頂きましょう」もある。この3つのうち、どの意味をさすのかは、そのときの状況、話す人のいい回し、前後のことばの関連で決まってくる。

　意味に3つあることから、こんな軽い冗談も生まれる。招待した家の奥さんが「もう少しいかがですか」と勧める。お客は答える。「結構です。」もう十分ごちそうになった、という意味である。それを承知のうえで奥さんが切り返す。「結構(delicious)でしたら、もっとお上がり下さらなくっちゃ。」

　食事の席でつかうだけではない。どんなときでも次の3つの意味でつかってよい。「よい」(good)とか「立派」(fine)、「十分に頂いたので満足している」(I've had enough, I'm satisfied)、それに「喜んで」(with pleasure)である。

Zensho shimasu

ZENSHO SHIMASU

Zensho shimasu is an expression with an affirmative positive tone: 'I shall do my best to respond to your wishes', or 'I shall deal with it accordingly', or 'I'll fix it up for you'. It is a widely used expression in business and in life in general.

If you point out to a customer that he has not been paying his bills regularly, he will say, *'zensho shimasu'*. If you complain that a manufacturer has been sending you substandard goods he will say, *'zensho shimasu'*.

It should be noted that the expression does not commit the speaker to a concrete course of action. It's a general 'I'll do my best'. That may sound reassuring, but do not assume that action will be taken.

善処します

　「善処します」とは「貴意に沿うよう最善を尽くします」(I shall do my best to respond to your wishes.) とか「適当に処理します」(I shall deal with it accordingly.) とか「しかるべく留意します」(I'll attend to it in a suitable manner.) とか「なんとか取り決めてあげましょう」(I'll fix it up for you.) のように肯定的で前向きのニュアンスをこめたことばである。仕事の話でも、日常一般でも、広くつかわれる。

　製造業者から送ってきた品物が規格外れだった。文句をつけると「善処します」。

　ここで注意すべきことは、この表現には、どうこうするという具体的行為をなにも約束していないことである。一般的に「最善を尽くします」というだけである。「善処します」と聞いて、やれ安心と思っても、約束どおりの措置がさっぱりとられていない。どうしたのかと聞く。まず一様に答えが返ってくる。「最善は尽くしたのですが、どうも……」

Gokurō-sama, otsukare-sama

GOKURŌ-SAMA, OTSUKARE-SAMA

The word *gokurō-sama* means 'I appreciate your labour' or 'Thank you for your trouble' or sometimes 'I sympathise with you for your tough assignment'. When the word is said to someone going off to do a job, it can carry the meaning of 'Good luck'. Thus it is an expression which can be used when a person is setting off to work, performing a task, has finished a job, or has returned from work.

Otsukare-sama is said to someone who has just completed a task. It means 'It must have been tiring', and expresses gratitude. The businessman returning from work is greeted by his wife with *otsukare-sama* or *gokurō-sama*.

Note how different this greeting is from the American housewife's 'What kind of day did you have?'

See SHITSUREI SHIMASU

CHOTTO

If you want to get a shop assistant to serve you, or get the waiter's attention in a restaurant, all you have to say is *chotto*. In the street, if you want to ask a stranger the way, your opening gambit can be *chotto*.

For the Japanese, it would be impolite to accost a stranger in the street with *chotto*. But for the visitor from abroad, it is not only acceptable but also somewhat charming if it is said in a genial or forlorn way.

Gokurō-sama, otsukare-sama

ご苦労さま，お疲れさま

「ご苦労さま」とは，"I appreciate your labor" とか "Thank you for your trouble" ときには "sympathize with you for your tough assignment" の意味である。これから仕事にとりかかろうという人にいうときには，"Good luck" の意味ともなる。つまり，これから仕事を始める人，仕事をしている最中の人，仕事を終えた人，あるいは勤めから帰宅した人など，いろいろにつかわれる。

「お疲れさま」は仕事を終えた人にいう。"It must have been tiring" の意味で，感謝をあらわす。勤めを終えて帰宅した夫に，妻は「お疲れさま」あるいは「ご苦労さま」とことばをかける。

→失礼します

ちょっと

お店で店員を呼びたいとき，レストランで給仕にきてもらいたいとき，「さて，なんといったらよいのか？」などとあれこれ思い悩むことはない。「ちょっと」といえば，万事こと足りる。見知らぬ人に道を尋ねるときまず最初に「ちょっと」である。

日本人が表で見も知らぬ人に「ちょっと」と呼びかけるのは失礼になることもある。しかし外国から来た人ならか

For another reason, also, *chotto* is one of the first words that anyone coming to Japan would learn. *Chotto matte* is 'One moment please!' or 'Wait!'. The polite way to say 'Please wait' is *chotto matte kudasai*.

See SUMIMASEN

KAO

Kao is 'face'. It is a vital word and concept in Japanese life. The uses of the word reveal a great deal of the Japanese character, as it does with the Chinese. It is most important for a foreign businessman to understand the many moods and feelings which *kao* can express.

The best-known of these expressions is, of course, 'to give face' or 'to save face': *kao wo tateru*. Extended meanings of this can be 'for your sake' and 'to prevent one from disgrace or dishonour'. Because consideration for the other party's honour and reputation is all-important in Japanese human relations, this expression is heard all the time. The opposite of 'to give one face' is *kao wo tsubusu* (to cause a loss of face).

In doing business it is an advantage to be a person

まわない。それどころか、やんわりと、明るく、あるいは困った表情でいえば、チャーミングでさえある。また、別の理由から、海外から日本に来た人が最初に覚えることばのひとつも「ちょっと」である。「ちょっと待て」は "one moment please" ないし "wait" で、電話でもほかでもつかえる重宝なことばである。

→すみません

顔

「顔」（face）は、国の如何を問わず、商売にはきわめて重要である。日本人が顔を重んじることは、顔を使った表現がたくさんあることでもわかる。

その第1は、なんといっても「顔を立てる」（to give face とか to save face）である。これを拡大して for your sake（あなたのために）とか to prevent one from disgrace or dishonor（不名誉なことにならないように）という意味になる。相手の名誉や評判を損なわないよう気を遣うことが、日本の人間関係ではとても大事なので、このことばはよく聞かれる。顔を立てるの反対は「顔をつぶす」である。

仕事をするには「顔が広い」（a person who has many

Kao

whose face is wide (*kao ga hiroi*) – in other words, a person with many contacts. A person who has many contacts is constantly doing things to 'keep his face in contact' (*kao wo tsunagu*), to maintain contacts which one has. He might do so by casually dropping into the other person's office from time to time, inviting him to lunch or to a game of golf, sending him gifts at the midsummer and year-end gift-giving sessions, and never failing to send New Year greetings.

Having many contacts with ordinary people isn't as useful as knowing people whose *kao ga kiku*. These are people with influence whose word goes a long way.

The Japanese also say *kao wo uru*, the direct translation of which is 'to sell face'. It means to 'sell' or 'advertise' oneself.

The face can also be 'loaned', as in the expression *kao wo kasu*. 'Lend me your face' is another usage which means 'I want to have a talk with you'. One is immediately reminded of Shakespeare's 'Lend me your ears'.

Many of the face expressions are used in the underworld, these being *kao wo uru* and *kao wo kasu*, for example.

contacts）と都合がいい。たくさんの"コネ"があり，顔が広い人は，「顔をつなぐ」(keep up contacts already made) ことに平常からつとめている。知人のオフィスにときどきぶらりと立ち寄る，昼めしやゴルフに誘う，盆暮れには付け届をする，年賀状を欠かさないなど。

普通の人との"コネ"をいくらたくさんもっていても，「顔のきく人」を知っていることには敵わない。顔のきく人とはそのことばに千金の重みがある実力者のことである。

「顔を売る」というのもある。直訳して sell the face といった方が，自分を売り込む(sell oneself, advertise oneself) のことだな，とすぐわかる。

顔は貸す (loan) こともできる。「ちょっと顔を貸せ」(Lend me your face) といえば,「話したいことがある」(I want to have a talk with you.) といった意味である。

ただし顔に関するいいまわしは，たくさんあるが，多くは，"やくざ"の陰語とみなされている。「顔を売る」「顔を貸す」などは，特にこの意味あいが強い。

JIN-MYAKU

This is a newly coined word which is not found in dictionaries but is widely used and aptly expresses one of the vital factors of Japanese life. *Jin* means 'man', 'person', 'human being'. *Myaku* means 'vein', as in a vein of mineral deposits. It also means the 'pulse', the 'heartbeat'. The closest English equivalent of *jin-myaku* is 'personal connections'. A freer translation could be 'the pulse of human contact'.

The Japanese are cool toward people they have not met before. But it is easy to thaw a Japanese if you know his *jin-myaku*. An introduction from anyone in his *jin-myaku* works like magic, swiftly and easily opening doors which reason, persuasion or argument could not open.

The building up of *jin-myaku* is a lifetime process, beginning in one's schooldays. A large *jin-myaku* is probably the biggest asset of the Japanese businessman, because human relationships are of paramount importance in Japanese society.

See BATSU

人脈

　新語で，和英辞典にはのっていないが，あらゆる仕事の分野で広く使われている。仕事をする上で重要な要因をうまく表現したことばである。「人」は man, person, human being の意。「脈」は "vein" as in a vein of mineral deposits（鉱脈のようにつかわれる）。一番近い英語は "personal connection" である。

　日本人は，知らない人には冷淡に対応する傾向がある。しかし，人脈を知っていれば，打ち解けやすい。その人の人脈につながる筋の紹介があれば，理屈や説得，議論ではどうにもならぬ門でも，まるで魔法のように，たちどころにあっさりと開くのである。

　人脈を築くことは，学校時代から始まって，一生の仕事である。人脈が広いことは，日本のビジネスマンにとっては最大の資産になる。日本の社会では，人間関係がなによりも重要だからである。

　→ 閥

Group orientation

A key characteristic of Japanese society that distinguishes it from the Western societies is the powerful group consciousness that pervades all aspects of Japanese life. The individual is suppressed in favour of the group and the forms and codes of behaviour of the group are of great importance.

To understand the Japanese, the strength of this centripetal force must be fully appreciated. The words and phrases that follow are expressions that illustrate these forces.

BATSU

Batsu typifies a characteristic of Japanese society: the emphasis on living, working and playing together in groups. *Batsu* is in fact an institution in Japan, and certainly is an essential part of the business organisational fabric.

Knowing what *batsu* a person belongs to facilitates the setting up of relations with him. In general terms *batsu* means 'clique', 'faction' or 'clan'.

There are various types of *batsu*. Major Japanese political parties often have factions (*ha-batsu*) which are like parties within the party. Each faction is constituted around an influential politician and is usually known by his name, e.g. Takahashi-*batsu*.

The *kei-batsu* is not necessarily an organised group as such, but it speaks with a loud voice. *Kei* literally means 'sleeping room'; it connotes wife and family. It is in a way a clan whose members are linked together by blood and marriage. People in the process of climbing up into the higher rungs of society through business success, political power or other means make every effort to get their sons and daughters married into high society: an arrangement which will be advantageous to them. This may appear like the social jostling in Western societies, but in Japan it is more directed to particular *batsu*.

The *gaku-batsu* is the alma-mater clique. If a young man joins a company where men from his university are dominant, *gaku-batsu* sectarianism will favour him in promotions. *Gaku* means 'education', 'learning'.

閥（ばつ）

「閥」は，日本社会の重要な仕組みである。その人がどの「閥」に属しているかを知っておくと，日本の社会で人間関係を良くするのに役立つ。一般に「閥」とは faction, clique ないし clan である。閥にもいろいろある。政党には「派閥」（ faction ）があり，党内党（ parties within the party ）のようなものである。派閥は勢力ある政治家を中心にした集まりで，その人の名を冠するのが普通である。

「閨閥」は，必ずしも「閥」として組織だったものではないが，やはり大きな影響力をもつ一族といってよい。血縁や姻戚関係（ linked by blood and marriage ）で結ばれている人びとである。事業で成功したり，政治権力その他の手段で社会の階層を昇りつめていく過程にある人びとは，自分の子女を良い家系に縁付かせようと必死になる。そうなってくれれば，万事好都合だからだ。

「学閥」は，同窓生仲間で作られる。新人の入った会社で，その出身大学の先輩が"幅"を利かしていれば，その人の昇進に有利となる。一方，その人の学閥が社内で勢力が小

Senpai and kōhai

On the other hand, if a person belongs to a minor *gaku-batsu* in the company, he has no chance of rising to a high executive position no matter how able he may be. In recent years, the *gaku-batsu* element has become less important in the business world, although it is still strongly entrenched in academic circles.

Another one is *chihō-batsu*. This can be regarded as a form of sectionalism because *chihō* is a word meaning 'district' or 'region'. Those who come from the same region of the country are regarded as belonging to the *batsu* of the area, and they tend to help and favour each other. However, thanks to the high demographic mobility of recent years, people are beginning to place less emphasis on this *batsu*.

SENPAI and KŌHAI

The same sense of belonging to a group that welded the old *batsu* is found in the 'old school tie' type of relationship.

In the Japanese business world, one of the gambits used to influence a person is to approach him through his *senpai*. *Senpai* is a person who was one's senior in school, in joining a company or government service, in assuming a post, in acquiring experience, etc. *Kōhai* is someone who follows in the footsteps of the *senpai*.

In Japan's seniority-conscious and paternalistic society, the *senpai-kōhai* relationship is of great importance. The *senpai* looks after the interests of the *kōhai*

さければ，どんなに有能でも，上級管理職に昇進する見込みはまずない。しかし近年は，学閥もビジネスの世界ではそれほど決定的な要素ではなくなってきている。しかし，官界や学界では，まだ根強いようだ。

「地方閥」というものもある。この閥は一種の sectionalism と思われる。同じ地方出身者は，地方閥に属しているとみなされ，これらの人達は，たがいに助けあい，便宜をはかる。だが，近年は人口流動が激しいので，この閥もだんだん重視されなくなってきた。

先輩と後輩

仕事の世界で，ある人に働きかけようとする場合に，まず，その人の「先輩」を通じてアプローチをするという手がつかわれる。「先輩」とは，学校の卒業年次とか，入社，入省，あるいは役職就任や経験の取得などで，相手よりも早い人をいう。「後輩」は先輩の歩んだ道をたどっている人である。

日本のように，年功序列の意識がつよく，家族主義的な社会では，先輩・後輩の関係はきわめて大切である。先輩は後輩の面倒をみる。

後輩は先輩の助けや忠言を仰ぎ，その意思を尊重する。

Dōsōsei

and the latter seeks help and advice from the former and respects his wishes.

A generation or so ago, the *senpai-kōhai* relationship was viable even if the two sides had never met before. Nowadays, such a relationship is markedly not as strong if in fact the two men do not know each other personally.

See JIN-MYAKU

DŌSŌSEI

Old school relationships play an important role in the Japanese business and social world. The simple fact that two businessmen have known each other since college days, and had attended the same school, is often reason enough to open a new account between two firms, expedite contracts, or arrange the informal exchange of business tips which are otherwise difficult to obtain. Japanese businessmen therefore go to great pains to maintain their *dōsōsei* (alumni) network. Class reunions are held frequently and alumni bulletins are circulated to keep the old school ties together. This is an example of lateral relationships in Japanese business society, which is generally structured vertically.

See BATSU

30年ほど以前は、面識がなくても先輩・後輩の関係は生きていた。いまでは、先輩・後輩といっても、よく知らない間柄だと、その関係はかなり薄くなってしまった。

→人脈

同窓生

日本では、学生時代の関係が、仕事の面でもつきあいの上でも、重要な役割を果たす。商談で2人が、たまたま大学時代からずっと知っているとか、同じ学校の「同窓生」だと分かると、それだけで会社同士の新しい取引に道が開けたり、買付契約がすらすら運んだり、ふつうならなかなか手に入らないビジネス上の情報も非公式に交換できる。だから日本のビジネスマンは、なんとかして「同窓生」(alumni) のつながりを保っておこうとする。昔の学校時代のきずなを断たないように、クラス会がひんぱんに開かれ、同窓会報も配布される。日本のビジネス社会は、本来タテ型の構造になりがちだが、これはヨコ型の関係の一例である。

→閥

ISHIN-DENSHIN

Ishin-denshin is the communication of thought without the use of words. The expression means 'What the mind thinks, the heart transmits.' In other societies, communication generally has to be expressed in specific words to be thoroughly understood. To the Westerner, therefore, the Japanese sometimes seem to possess telepathic powers because so often communication among Japanese is achieved without the use of words.

This is because the many formalities, conventions and common standards developed in a society which gives priority to harmonious relations makes it easy to understand what goes on in the mind of the other person.

The younger generation of Japanese who have become more individualistic are losing the *ishin-denshin* faculty.

See HARA-GEI

以心伝心

「以心伝心」とは、ことばを用いずに腹のうちを相手に伝えることをいう。"What the mind thinks, the heart transmits"の意味である。ほかの社会、とりわけ西洋では、理解を十分にはかるため、明確なことばで表現して、コミュニケートするのがふつうである。だから、西洋の人からみると、日本人は霊感をもっているのではないか、と思ったりする。ことばを用いずにコミュニケートできるからである。

ことばをつかわずに分かりあえるのは、日本の社会の定まりごと、しきたり、共通の基準といったものが、事を荒立てぬをもって旨としているので、相手の心の内の動きを読めるからである。日本人でも、若い世代は、だんだんと個人主義的になってきたので「以心伝心」の霊感を失いつつあるようだ。

→腹芸

Suri-awase

SURI-AWASE

If you push a new Japanese teacup or bowl across a table, it would scratch the surface of the table, because the rim on the underside of the chinaware is not glazed. Therefore, whenever Japanese housewives buy new chinaware they rub the bottom rims of two bowls together. This is known as *suri-awase*.

The word was taken from this original usage to describe the process of adjusting different viewpoints among members of a group through mutual concession and through unifying the opinions of the group into a co-ordinated whole. Similarly, the adjustment of views between different groups is also sometimes called *suri-awase*. The process of jelling of a group's views is also called *nemawashi*. The conciliation of views of different groups is a sort of bargaining process. The prerequisite in both cases is that the differences should not be too great, as the original term means 'rubbing the bottoms *of the same kind of bowl*'.

The word *suri-awase* is used for political discussions and settlements, but is not used in the diplomatic world.

See NEMAWASHI

Suri-awase

すりあわせ

　湯呑み茶椀の糸底は，上薬がかけられていないものがあり，うっかり卓上に置くと，机の表面を傷つけてしまうことがある。だから，新しい陶器を買ってきたら，まず糸底同士を「すりあわせ」て，机などを傷つけないようにしなければならない。

　このことから，グループ内メンバー個々の意見の相違点を調整し，相互に譲歩しながらグループ全体の意見一致を図ることを「すりあわせ」と呼んでいる。またグループ相互間の意見調整も「すりあわせ」ということもある。前者は根回しともいえるし，後者は交渉事ともいえようが，いずれにしろ，同じ茶椀の底をすりあわせるように，もともとあまり大きな相違点のないことが前提だろう。

　政治用語としても使われるこのことばは，せいぜい党内意見調整程度で，外交用語としては無理なようである。

　→根回し

Uogokoro areba mizugokoro

UOGOKORO AREBA MIZUGOKORO

Whereas *suri-awase* suggests that both sides need to adjust their respective viewpoints to reach a decision, the proverb *uogokoro areba mizugokoro* refers to those human relationships which are somewhat more congenial. It means that if one side should display a favourable feeling, the other side would respond in the same spirit. It is most often used in connection with male-female relationships.

A rough translation of the proverb would be: If the fish has a heart for the water, the water will have heart for the fish. It expresses like-mindedness or compatibility. In the business world it can be used to show a give-and-take relationship.

The essence can be found in the English saying, 'Scratch my back, and I'll scratch yours,' which is the same thing, but with a little less delicacy.

Uogokoro areba mizugokoro

魚心あれば水心

　これは男女の間柄をいうときによく使われる諺(proverb)である。本人に憎からず思っている気持ちがあれば、相手にもそれに応えようとする気持ちがあることの意。

　ことばどおりに訳すと、"If the fish has the heart for the water, the water will have heart for the fish." 似たような気持ちのあること、とか、気持ちが合致することをいう。商売の世界でいうと、"give-and-take"(互いに譲りあう)の関係をいう。

　英語にもこれに似た諺がある。"Roll my log and I'll roll yours."(こっちの丸太をころがしてくれ、そうしたら、そっちの丸太もころがしてやろう) "Scratch my back and I'll scratch yours."(こっちの背中を掻いてくれ、そしたら君の背中も掻いてあげるから) "Do as you would be done by."(君がしてほしいことを人にしてあげなさい)

Individuality

Given the deep centripetal force of Japanese society and the dominant facade of group discipline one tends to overlook individuality in the Japanese. Actually the conflict between the individual and the group does exist as much in Japan as it does in other societies. Today, as external influences creep into the traditional society, the conflict of the individual versus the group is growing.

In the notes that follow we shall be dealing with words that reveal some of these problems.

RŌNIN

In the feudal times there were some hapless individuals among the samurai. These were the *rōnin*.

Rōnin were the samurai who, for one reason or another, were not in the service of a lord. Thus the word is usually translated as 'masterless samurai'. Today, a century after the samurai have disappeared, there are still many *rōnin* in Japanese society.

One type of modern-day *rōnin* is the high-school graduate who fails to pass a university entrance examination and studies privately before trying his luck again the following year. There are tens of thousands of such youngsters, some of whom have been *rōnin* for two or three years.

Another type of *rōnin* is the person who is unemployed, not because no company will hire him, but because he is particular about the kind of work he wants to do, and is voluntarily unemployed.

Politicians who have lost an election and who are preparing to run in the next one are also called *rōnin*.

浪人

「浪人」は、封建時代になんらかの理由で仕官していないサムライをいう。訳せば masterless samurai（主君なきサムライ）というところか。サムライがいなくなった現代でも、日本にはまだ浪人がたくさんいる。

高校は出たけれど大学入試に失敗、来年に捲土重来を期して、ひとり勉強している学生も浪人である。こうした若者は何万といて、なかには2年、3年と浪人をつづけるものもいる。

もうひとつの浪人は、意に染まぬ仕事はしたくない、などの理由でみずから好んで"失業中"のばあいである。選挙に落ちて、次期出馬に備えている政治家もやはり浪人である。

GOMASURI

You will find him in every organisation and every society. He may not be a bad fellow but his colleagues do not speak well of him. More often than not he is looked upon with contempt, except by the person on whom he directs his charm.

In the English-speaking world, the *gomasuri* is known as the 'apple polisher', 'the one who licks the boss's boots', 'teacher's pet', 'the sycophant' ... a self-seeking person who courts favour by flattery and obvious servility. The literal translation of *gomasuri* is 'a person who grinds the sesame seeds'.

Roasted sesame seeds are ground in an earthenware mortar to make flavourings in Japanese food. In the grinding process, the seeds stick to the wall of the mortar, just as the one who tries to curry favour clings to the boss.

ごますり

　この種の人間は，どの組織，どの社会にもいる。悪い奴ではないのだろうが，彼のことを同僚はよくいわない　たいていは軽蔑の眼でみられる。ごまをすられている人は別だ。英語圏では，「ごますり」は apple polisher である。おおげさにいえば sycophant のこと。つまり相手におべっかをつかって，卑屈な態度で気に入られようとする利己主義者のこと。「ごますり」を直訳すると a person who grinds sesame seeds ということになる。

　日本料理に風味をつけるため，煎った「ごま」をすりばちですって利用する。この「ごま」は，すられているうちに，種子が四方に散って，すり鉢の内壁にべったりと付着する。

　このように，名詞は「ごますり」── apple polisher とか apple polishing。動詞の「ごまをする」は，to flatter or toady となる。

Konjō

KONJŌ

A businessman who is described as *konjō ga aru* (possessing *konjō*) is one who has fighting spirit, will power, determination and guts. He is a person who gets things done even against great odds. Adversity never gets him down. In fact adversity spurs him to greater efforts. He is a tough negotiator who never gives up. The opposite is *konjō ga nai*.

To his boss, the *konjō ga aru* subordinate is one who can be trusted to carry out the most difficult assignment without a word of complaint. The boss does not have to keep looking over his shoulder. *Konjō* is that extra element, aside from expertise or experience, that makes a man stand out from the crowd.

根性

　あの人は「根性がある」といえば、「闘志、意思力、決意、辛抱強さ、度胸」のある人である。条件が悪いのに立派に事を成し遂げる人のことである。逆境にあって挫けない人のことである。それどころか、逆境に立つと、かえって勇気百倍する人である。交渉相手としては、タフである。絶対に諦めない。「根性がある」の反対は「根性がない」。

　上司にとって根性がある部下は頼りになる。どんなにむずかしい仕事でも、文句ひとついわずにやってくれるからだ。肩ごしにいちいち点検したり、はっぱをかけたりする必要はない。だから、ビジネスマンにとって、「根性」は、専門知識とか経験とは別に、特別の資質であり、その人の値打ちを高めるものである。

KOGAI

Kogai means 'a pet', or 'keeping a pet'. The word later came to be used to refer to a person who apprenticed himself as a child to a merchant or artisan under the old teacher-disciple system. Today a person who receives the favours and patronage of a superior under whom he has served since joining the company is called the *kogai* of that superior. Such a person would be a devoted and trusted subordinate.

The contrasting word is *tozama*. The word which originally was the opposite of *tozama* was *fudai* which referred to a hereditary vassal or one of successive generations of the same family serving under a feudal family. The latter word is hardly ever used today as the days of serfs and servile families have gone.

See TOZAMA

子飼い

　本来は，犬猫など，子どもから飼い育てるペット，またはそのような飼い方をいう。転じて少年のころから弟子として働く徒弟制度下の商人，職人のことを指す。現代では新入社員当時から一定の上司に仕え，可愛がられ，引き立てられているようなばあい「彼はＡ氏の子飼いだ」などという。信頼されている腹心の部下の意味になる。

　対することばは「外様」だが，もともと外様と対比されることば「譜代」は，ビジネス社会ではあまり使われない。特定の領主家に代々仕えてきた家臣を譜代の臣と呼ぶのだが，現代では特定企業に代々勤めるなどは稀であり，まして特定の人に親子とも部下になることなどは無いからだろうか。

→ 外様

HIRU-ANDON

Hiru-andon is translated as 'a lamp in daylight'. In broad daylight one cannot tell whether the lamp has been lit or not. Thus the word is used to describe a person whose presence or existence is not important, or to describe a person who is difficult to assess. However it does not mean a person who is slow to react, or who is mediocre. (A person who is slow to react is called a *keikōtō*, after the fluorescent lamp which takes time to light up.)

A Japanese organisation often operates better when it is headed by a person who does not stand out, but has a sharp and quick second-in-command. With such a team, the top man will function admirably as the symbolic head, while his second-in-command carries the responsibility.

Often, there are several deputies and staff officers, so power is seldom concentrated in one man. This approach to organisation together with the spirit of group responsibility prevents dictatorial control of the company.

Hiru-andon, the lamp shining unseen in the sunlight, is therefore not necessarily a pejorative term.

昼あんどん

　日中の「あんどん」の意味である。陽光下での「あんどん」は灯いているかいないかわからないところから，その人の存在価値が重視されないような人，またはその人の真価があるのかないのか解らない人のことをいう。ただし反応の遅い人（点灯の遅いところから「蛍光灯」という）とか，凡愚の人の意味ではない。

　日本の組織では，このように一見ぼんやりとした様子の人を長とし，有能な「切れ者」を懐刀ないし参謀として運営すると，ことがうまく運ぶことが多い。このばあいトップは象徴であり，副ないし参謀が結果についての責任を負うことになるし，副ないし参謀も複数であることが多いから，特定個人に権力が集中することは少ない。すなわち独裁者が生まれないのは，こうした組織感覚が日本には昔からあったからであろう。

　したがって「昼あんどん」とは，かならずしも人をおとしめたことにもならないし，「切れ者」は，かならずしも褒めたことばとはならないのである。

Futokoro-gatana

FUTOKORO-GATANA

To say a man is like a dagger in Japanese is not an uncomplimentary remark. The original meaning of *futokoro-gatana* is that of a dagger. It would be regarded as a compliment if you said so-and-so was a *futokoro-gatana*, for it means a confidant or right-hand man.

The meaning comes from feudal Japan when a knife *(gatana)* was carried at the breast *(futokoro)*. It was the instrument used for *hara-kiri*, with which a man could defend his honour if necessary.

From this the word assumed the contemporary meaning of a man who is in on the secret plans of an important person, or one who is trusted by the boss. *Futokoro-gatana* is also a sort of chief of staff or a right-hand man.

Kiremono is another word for 'knife'. Literally, 'a cutting thing'. *Kiremono* is used to describe a sharp and able man. Again, a complimentary term in Japanese, which does not have the connotations of a 'sharpie' or a 'hatchet man' as it does in English.

Futokoro-gatana

懐刀（ふところがたな）

英語圏で，人をあいくちなどにたとえても，あまり褒めたことにならないだろう。もともと「懐刀」とは，あいくちとか短刀のことだが，日本では，これになぞらえられると重要視されたことになる。人に対しては腹心の部下とか右腕の意味でつかわれるからである。これは，封建時代の日本で「懐」（bosom）に短刀を携えていたところからきたものである。この短刀は，名誉を護るために切腹するときの道具でもあった。

ここから，「懐刀」ということばは今日一般につかわれている。責任ある地位の人の内密な計画を知っている人，またはこのような責任ある人に信用されている腹心的存在の人を指す。いいかえれば，「懐刀」とは，偉い人の参謀またはブレインといった役どころの人である。

Hijikake-isu

HIJIKAKE-ISU

Hijikake-isu illustrates the hidden individualism and subtle shades of strata in the vertical structure of Japanese companies.

When you walk into a Japanese office, you can tell who ranks above whom by the type of chair they are sitting in. The chair most coveted by company employees is the *hijikake-isu*, a large one with arm rests. The rank and file sit in the simplest, functional office chairs. They are not chairs for resting in but for working.

When a man is promoted to the first rung of the managerial ladder, he gets a chair with arm rests and quite often a bigger desk. As he goes up the ladder, he is given an increasingly larger and more comfortable *hijikake-isu*. When he gets to the leather-upholstered chair with a high back, he is a director or perhaps the president. The *hijikake-isu* is a chair for sinking into and thinking.

Similar differences can be found in the Western corporate system, but the fine steps in grades of chairs and the importance attached to these status symbols can be observed to be of far greater significance in Japan.

肱かけ椅子

　日本のオフィスに入ると、座っている人の椅子をみれば、どの人がどの人より偉いか、すぐ分かる。サラリーマンが一度は座りたいと思っているのが、肱かけ椅子である。平社員はもっとも機能的な事務椅子に座る。休憩する椅子ではなく、働く椅子である。

　管理職への階段の第1段を昇ると、肱かけがついた椅子と、しばしば今迄より一回り大きい机が与えられる。昇進してゆくにつれて、肱かけ椅子はだんだんと大きく、座り心地のいいものになってゆく。皮張りで、うしろに寄りかかれる椅子に手が届いたときには、重役か社長である。どっかりとよりかかり、物を考える椅子である。

KUBI

Japanese in responsible positions are fond of the expression *kubi wo kakate,* meaning 'stake my neck'. The neck is a personal thing: a symbol of position, honour, reputation or even life. *Kubi wo kakete* is an expression of confidence and determination in undertaking some big task.

Actually, in a Japanese organisation, it is pretty safe to 'stake one's neck' on anything, because under the lifetime employment system it is rare that one is ever fired (*kubi ga tobu*: the neck flies). This is not to say that companies never carry out staff reduction (*kubikiri*: cutting necks), because under extreme pressure any company has to scale down to survive.

When a company or an individual finds itself deep in debt (*kubi ga mawaranai*: cannot turn the neck), it has to think hard (*kubi wo hineru*: wring the neck) and to devise ways to get out of the mess.

A euphemistic Japanese expression which uses the word *kubi* is *mawata de kubi wo shimeru*. The last part of this translates as 'strangle the neck'. *Mawata* is a delicate silk floss which is soft on the skin. Strangling with such a silk floss means using a gentle or indirect way to throttle a person gradually. It is used to describe an operation for easing someone out by making it impossible for him to stay.

首

　責任ある地位にいる人がよく「首をかけて」という。"stake my neck" のこと。この neck（首）は地位とか名誉, 評判ないし生命そのものを指す。なにか大仕事に取り組むときに自信と決意のほどを示すことばである。

　もちろん, 日本の会社では首をかけたところで心配はいらない。終身雇用制だから,「首がとぶ」(to be fired) ことはまずない。終身雇用制でも, 会社側が「首切り」(personnel reduction) を絶対にやらないわけではない。極度の営業不振になって, 会社が生き残るには業務の縮小に追い詰められることもある。

　会社でも個人でも, 借金に首までつかっているとき, つまり「首が回らない」(cannot turn the neck) とき, 打開策はないかと「首をひねる」(wring the neck, または rack the brain = 頭をしぼる。think hard = 一所懸命考える)。

　首をつかった婉曲ないい回しに「真綿で首をしめる」がある。首をしめるは "strangle the neck", 真綿は肌にやさしいくず絹 (silk floss)。真綿で首をしめるとは, おだやかな方法, 間接的なやり方で人の首を徐々に締めつけていくことをいう。だんだんと窮地に追いこんで, ついにはいられなくなるように仕向けることである。

KUROMAKU

The first character of this two-character phrase is the Chinese character for 'black'; and the second, the character for 'curtain'. In the old days the backdrop to a stage was always a black curtain. Today, when a person is called a *kuromaku*, he is an influential man behind the scenes, the string-puller who does not hold an official post.

Such people abound in every society, mostly in politics, sometimes with sinister intentions. In the Japanese business world, *kuromaku* are not found in individual corporations but in a particular industry as a whole.

黒幕

「黒幕」の「黒」は black,「幕」は curtain。昔,舞台の背景幕としてつかわれたもの。現代では,黒幕とは,舞台裏にあって影響力をもっている人,表から見えないところで操る人,表向きのポストに就いてない人をいう。

この種の人物は,どの社会にもいる。とりわけ政界に多い。あまりいい意味に使われない場合もある。ビジネスの世界となると,個々の会社にはいなくても,その業界全体をみたとき,影響力のある黒幕がいることはある。

ŌGOSHO, INSEI

Originally *ōgosho* meant the residence of a retired shogun (feudal military governor), and *insei* the system under which a retired emperor continued to rule. Today the former term is used to mean the most prominent and influential figure, the 'grand old man' in a sector of society: for example, in industry, medicine, sports. The *ōgosho* is universally recognised as being a man of great stature. He may be retired or may still be active.

Insei today refers to a situation in which a person continues to wield great power in an organisation or field of activity from which he has already retired. He is able to do this because his successor is weak and is dependent on him, or because he had successfully built up a very strong personal power base before officially retiring from the post.

Japanese history is strewn with *insei* in many different fields.

大御所，院政

　もともと，「大御所」とは隠居した公卿や将軍のいる所から，その人への尊称となった。「院政」とは，退位した天皇がなお政治を執ること。いまは，「大御所」というと，もっとも卓越した，勢力ある人物。組織やある種の業界——実業界，文学・医学・スポーツ界などで，その道の長老をさす。大御所は，衆目の一致するところ，文句なしの人物で，現役か否かはとくに関係ない。

　院政は，もう隠退したのに，組織なり，その道でなお大きな勢力を振るっていること。後任者が弱体で，その人を頼りにしているとか，在任中に権力基盤をがっちり築き上げてしまったため，引退後もなお実力を残しているようなばあいである。

NEWAZA-SHI

Newaza-shi is a person who is skilled in behind-the-scenes negotiations. This is not quite the same as a *kuromaku*. A *newaza-shi* does not move in the high political circles and *zaibatsu* circuits as a *kuromaku* does. A *newaza-shi* springs surprises. The term comes from the judo term *newaza*, which is an offensive technique used by the contestant lying on the mat. *Ne* in the word means sleep.

With his multitude of devices, a *newaza-shi* often engineers an unexpected reversal which completely changes the complexion of things. At other times with his clandestine manoeuvrings, he makes possible what seemed impossible to those operating up in front. A *newaza-shi* can always be relied on to spring a surprise.

TOZAMA

Tozama is a word which is symbolic of the structure of Japanese society.

In the feudal days, it was customary to enter the lord's service at a very early age and serve for life, or for a son to follow his father's footsteps as a retainer to the same lord. Anyone who did not enter the lord's service in these traditional ways was called a *tozama* (an outside person, an outsider).

Today, a person who is hired by a company not straight out of school but after some years in another

寝わざ師

　舞台裏の駆け引きにたけた人を「寝わざ師」という。柔道の寝技からきたことば。試合で，畳に寝たような状態で相手を攻める技（わざ）である。

　これから分かるように，寝わざ師は，豊富な術策を用いて，しばしば，物事の情況を完全に変えてしまうような，思いがけない逆転をもたらす。また，秘密の策動をして，表面でそれにたずさわっている人には不可能と思われることを可能にする。

　「あの人は寝わざ師だ」という評判があるなら，その人は，意表をつくようなことをするだろうと期待できる。

外様

　「外様」とは，日本の社会の仕組みを象徴的にあらわすことばである。直訳すると outside person とか outsiderとなる。

　封建時代には，幼少から藩主に仕え，一生同一藩主に仕えるのが当たり前であった。また，その子息も父親の仕える藩主に仕え，父親同様一生同じ藩に属することとなっていた。これが「譜代」の侍であり，一方扶持を離れた浪人が，途中から他家へ仕えたばあいは「外様」と呼ばれた。

Mai hōmu

organisation is a *tozama*. In Japan's vertical society, a *tozama* is one who is not 'purebred'.

An *ama-kudari* is literally one who has descended from heaven. It is applied to someone who comes in to head a division from outside the division, perhaps from a subsidiary of the main company or from a government ministry. He is a special kind of *tozama*.

MAI HŌMU

The Japanese businessman is generally thought of as an eager beaver employee racing frenziedly up the corporate ladder. He works like a madman all day long, sacrificing time which a businessman in any other country would be spending with his family. He does not use up his annual leave, because he believes he is so indispensable to the company's day-to-day operations that he must be at the office all the time. And his bosses encourage this attitude.

A generation ago, this description applied to almost all Japanese. But not everybody is a workaholic these days. More and more businessmen of the younger generation are having second thoughts about the traditional values. They value family life as much as their career. The number of this new breed has increased so much that a new expression has been coined for such people. This is an expression borrowed from the English 'my home' and twisted slightly: *mai-hōmu-shugisha*, 'a follower of the "my home" principle'.

今日、学校を出ると同時に入社するのでなく、何年間か他の会社に勤めてから中途入社した者が「外様」といわれている。天下りしてくる人も同様に外様である。日本のタテ社会では、生え抜きでないものは、すべて外様と呼ばれる。

マイホーム

日本の勤め人というと、会社の出世街道にのろうと、ひたすらに働く人間のように思われている。日がな1日、他の国なら家族団らんの時間なのにそれまで犠牲にして、ただあくせくと働く。有給休暇があるのに、とらない。自分がいないことには毎日の仕事がはかどらない、だからいつも出社していなければ、と思いこむ。

一世代まえの勤め人は、だれもがそんな風だった。ところが近頃は、皆が皆、働き中毒ということはなくなった。若い世代の勤め人は、これまでの価値観を考え直すようになっている。仕事と同じくらいに、いやそれ以上に、家庭生活も大事にするようになった。そうした人達がふえているところから生まれた新語が「マイホーム主義者」(my - home - ist) である。

Social and business fabric

We move on from the words that refer to individuals to a variety of expressions that together show us different facets of Japanese society, and of Japanese business. All these words are used frequently in business and reveal attitudes and approaches. Some of them, like *go-en* and *giri*, describe basic concepts that have general applications, while words like *apointo* and *gashi-kōkan* are special words of the commercial world.

Go-en

GO-EN

Go-en is a concept that is not easy to comprehend. *En* is a Buddhist term. In Buddhism, there is a cause to all things. The medium through which the cause is brought into effect is *en*. *En* can be interpreted as part of the relationship chain of the cause, the *en*, and the effect; the past, the *en*, and the future.

The relationship between man and woman, social intercourse with neighbours, with business partners, all begin and change with *en*. The word is generally used with the honorific prefix *go-en*. Thus *go-en* is a 'chance' or 'occasion'. *En ga aru* means 'to have a relationship'. The philosophy of *en* pervades Japanese society, and surfaces in many word forms. A foreigner should be aware of the concept even though he may never grasp the full import of *go-en*.

When one says, 'We have an *en* with that company', it means that his company has business with that company or that his company's staff may be bidding for the same tenders as that company and they are often together in the same place.

In daily life *en* is used in reference to a man-woman relationship. *Endan* is the discussion about arranging a marriage. *En wo kiru* is cutting off of the *en*, as when a couple break up.

ご　縁

「縁」とは仏教語。万物はすべて原因があって生まれるわけだが、その原因から結果を生む媒体が縁である。過去（因）、現在（縁）、未来（果）ともいえる。

男女の仲、近所の付き合い、取引先との付き合い、すべて縁があって始まる。この場合、「縁」丁寧にいって「ご縁」とは、機会であり、「縁がある」とは関係があるの意味となる。

「あの会社とは縁がある」といえば、その会社と当社とは取引があるか、競合関係にあって入札などに同席することが多いことなどを指す。

ただ日常で縁といえば、男女間の関係をいうことが多い。縁の話＝縁談とは、若い男女をもつ親のところにもちかける結婚の話で、縁があると夫婦になり、縁がないと結ばれない。「縁を切る」とは、夫婦の別れ、「金の切れ目が縁の切れ目」とは、遊里での愛情は金がなくなるとおしまいということ。

HON·NE and TATEMAE

'That man doesn't disclose his *hon·ne* (real intentions) easily,' is an expression Japanese businessmen use when talking about a tough negotiator on the other side of the table. The other party in a business negotiation may not be obstinate because he wants to be, but because, under certain circumstances, he has to emphasise his company's *tatemae* (principles or official stance).

When the *tatemae* and the *hon·ne* are one and the same, there is no problem, but sometimes they happen to be at variance with each other. The negotiation then becomes an exercise in trying to find a way to satisfy the *hon·ne* without compromising the *tatemae*, at least on the surface.

Excessive adherence to *tatemae*, of course, is often used as a ploy to gain a better bargaining position. The reluctance to reveal the *hon·ne* and to stick ostensibly to *tatemae* also occurs in private social relations, especially when the *hon·ne* is not a very laudable one.

本音と建前

"あの人はなかなか「本音」(real intentions)をいわない"とは、商談で手ごわい相手について日本のビジネスマンがつかう表現である。交渉相手は、なにもそうしたいから頑張っているのではなく、会社の「建前」(principles または official stance)を力説せねばならないために譲ろうとしないのである。

「建前」と「本音」が同じであれば、なにも問題はない。ところが往々にして、この2つが食い違っていることがある。そのばあい、少なくとも表面上は「建前」を崩さずに「本音」を満たす方策を見つけることが交渉術になる。もちろん、かけ引きの立場を有利にする手として、建前に過度にこだわることもある。本音を明かさずに、表面上、建前に固執するというのは、個人のつきあいでもよくあることだ。本音があまり見上げたものでないときは、よけいにその傾向がつよい。

Gebahyō

GEBAHYŌ

Although dictionaries give 'rumour' and 'gossip' as the English equivalents of the Japanese word *gebahyō*, it has nuances that embrace more than these equivalents.

It is frequently used to mean speculation among outsiders concerning the possible outcome of an event or proceedings, relating mostly to personnel matters. Thus, the *gebahyō* at Kabuto-cho (Japan's Wall Street) is that Mr A will be selected over Mr B as the next president of company X.

The origin of the word goes back to the days when retainers, waiting for their lords at the horse-dismounting place (*geba* is to dismount) outside a castle or shrine or temple, engaged in idle speculation over personnel changes in the Shogun government.

NOREN

In the old days, *noren*, a kind of cloth, cotton, rope or hemp curtain, was hung under the eaves of a house to keep out the sun. In the Edo period (17th to 19th century), merchants dyed their shop name on the *noren* and used it as a signboard.

The word thus came to mean not only the reputation of a store but also the business rights of the

下馬評

　ふつうの和英辞典で下馬評をひくと rumor とか gossip とある。しかし，このことばは，英語にないニュアンスでつかわれるのがふつうである。すなわち「これから起こることや行事ないし過程についてのうわさ話。ほとんどが人事関係のうわさ話」の意味につかう。だから「兜町（日本版ウォール街）の下馬評だと，X社の次期社長にはB氏を抜いてA氏が選任されるだろう」といったつかい方をする。語源は，江戸時代，城，神社，寺院の外の下馬地域で，供待ちが幕府高官の人事異動について，たわいもない臆測をしたことに溯る。

のれん（暖簾）

　軒先に吊して日よけ，目かくしとする布（しゅろ，麻を編んだ縄のれんもある）だが，江戸時代の商家で軒先に商店名（屋号）を染めて吊す店の看板であった。
　転じて店の信用や営業権などを意味するようになった。日本では契約の習慣が無かったようにみえるが，「のれん

establishment. Merchants began to say that they would stake their *noren* on a venture. The *noren* took on a symbolic meaning. To say that you stake your *noren* was as good as signing a written contract. Anyone who behaved in any way that soiled his *noren* was treated as unreliable and incompetent. The *noren* was in fact the merchant's 'face'. Today the *noren* represents a company's credit and even its social reputation.

In the old days it was the practice to divide the *noren* (*noren-wake*), which meant giving a clerk with long service a *noren* with the same mark and same name as the master's store to open a new shop. Sometimes the master gave the clerk some financial assistance to start up, and even passed some of his customers over to the new store, an arrangement similar to the franchise arrangement of today.

GAIJIN

If you stay in Japan you will soon learn that all foreigners are lumped together under the generic term of *gaijin*. *Gai* is 'outside'; *jin* is 'man'. You will be told that *gaijin* means 'foreigner'.

Originally, *gaijin* was used to mean 'outsiders': people outside one's circle, or people with whom one did not have much contact. And people from overseas naturally fell into this category.

にかけて……」の約束は，その商人の全人格・全信用を担保にしての契約ともいえるものであった。「のれんを汚す」行為は，現代では禁治産者扱いされるに等しい。正に，のれんは商人の顔であり，軍人にとっての軍旗であった。現在ではのれんに当たるものは，会社の信用，社会的評価などか。

なお，かつて「のれん分け」として古くからの番頭に同名・同印ののれんを与え，独立の分店を開かせることがあり，ばあいにより資金援助や得意先も分けることがあった。現代でのフランチャイザーとフランチャイジーに似ていよう。

外　人

本来外人とは，仲間以外の人とかあまり付き合いのない人のことで，また外国人一般をも意味するものであった。

鎖国時代の日本が常時交際する外国人はただの二つ，唐人（中国古代王朝唐の人の意から，転じて中国人の意）と夷人（オランダ人，夷とは野蛮の意）とであった。19世紀後半，欧米人がどっと入ってくるようになると，軽

Gaijin

During the 200 years of Japan's isolation from the rest of the world up to 1868, the only people the Japanese came into contact with were the Chinese and the Dutch. The Chinese were called *tōjin* (citizens of the Tang Dynasty) while the Dutch were called *i-jin*, the character for '*i*' meaning either 'barbarian' or 'different'. Different obviously in colour of hair, skin and eyes.

In the twentieth century, as more and more foreigners appeared in Japan, the word *i-jin* gave way to *ketō* (hairy *tōjin*), which carried a note of contempt. It was used by the ultra-nationalists. The word *gaijin* came into use only after Japan's defeat in the last war. This word has none of the derogatory connotations of the previous words used for foreigners. Today it carries the considerably bland meaning of 'non-Japanese', referring mainly to the Occidentals.

It is interesting to compare the words that the Japanese selected to refer to foreigners with the words the Chinese chose. The Chinese tried to be more precise and injected much greater antagonism in calling Westerners 'red-headed devils'; and today, in the Communist People's Republic of China, they have chosen to use a word as bland as the Japanese *gaijin*, but physically more precise: 'the big-nose ones'.

Gaijin

蔑の意味がある夷人では具合が悪くなって、異人と称するようになる。髪の色、眼の色、肌の色が異なる人の意味である。

欧米人がたくさん渡来する20世紀では、異人はすたれて毛唐（毛深い唐人＝外国人）という侮蔑的な言葉も使われた。これを敗戦後あらためて外人と呼ぶようになったので、ここには外国人を対等にみる精神が働いている。ただこの言葉の歴史が語るように、外人には東洋人を含まないニュアンスがあり、主に白人を指すのである。

Giri

GIRI

Giri is the linchpin of human relations among the Japanese. Essentially the word refers to the things which people must do, or the correct behaviour for smooth social interaction. Thus it covers a wide range of forms, attitudes and behaviour.

When someone says, 'I owe that man *giri*', he means that he has received some favour from him some time in the past and that he must eventually return the favour.

To repay a debt of gratitude is *giri wo hatasu*. Sending midsummer (*ochūgen*) and year-end (*oseibo*) gifts, and sending gifts on personal ceremonial occasions such as engagements, marriages, funerals, etc., is one way to *giri wo hatasu*. A person who meticulously observes such practices is a *giri-gatai hito* (a man who discharges his social duties faithfully). However, if such acts lack sincerity, he will be criticised as *giri ippen* or doing it without feeling.

Giri no naka refers to the relationships between one's in-laws and implies that one must treat one's in-laws as though they were blood relatives.

In a company, if either a senior or a subordinate forms a *giri ga karamu*, a *batsu* has started to jell.

See BATSU, ON

義 理

　社会生活を円満にすごすために人が行なうべきこと，正しい道といった意味だが，実に広い範囲で使われる。

　「あの人には義理がある」といえば，かつて世話になったことがあり，いずれお返しをしなければならない人，恩人のこと。

　「義理を果たす」はお返しをすること，また中元・歳暮などの付け届けや冠婚葬祭の交際上出費を果たすこと。これをキチンキチンとやる人は「義理がたい人」とほめられる。だが，そのお返しや交際に心がこもっていないと義理一遍（通り一遍）と，かえって悪評を受ける。

　「義理の仲」は，義父母，義兄弟など血族でないが，血族のような交際をしなければならない仲。

　会社のなかで，上司と部下・同輩間に「義理がからむ」と，そこには一つの閥＝人脈的結合ができたことになる。

　→閥，恩

Dame-oshi

DAME-OSHI

Dame-oshi means 'to make doubly sure'. You accept an invitation to a business dinner. On the day of the dinner, you get a call from your host's secretary to confirm your attendance. You promise to deliver goods on a certain date. A few days before the scheduled time, the customer inquires if he can still expect the goods on that date. A decision has been reached at a meeting. Some time later those who were at the meeting are asked to confirm the decision.

All these are examples of *dame-oshi*. This kind of perpetual reminding and reconfirmation is often irritating to a foreigner, but in Japanese society *dame-oshi* is an accepted practice which ensures that things will go smoothly as previously arranged, decided, or promised. *Dame-oshi* reduces the possibility of last-minute hitches, although students of management will argue whether it leads to greater efficiency or whether it is an unnecessary waste of effort.

A more descriptive phrase used to refer to 'make doubly sure' but with an implication of excessive caution is *kugi wo sasu*. This means 'to drive a nail into a carpenter's mortise and tenon joint'.

だめ押し

「だめ押し」は英語で "making something doubly sure" である。仕事の話で夕食会の招待を受けたとする。その当日，招待側の秘書から電話がかかってきて，出席をあらためて確認する。これこれの日に品物を届ける約束をする。配達予定日の2，3日前に，お客から約束の配達日に変更はないかどうか問いあわせてくる。会議である事項が決まった。しばらくして，この会議に出席した人達は，決定事項の再確認を求められる。

これらはすべて，だめ押しの例である。この種の注意喚起なり再確認は，欧米の人には煩雑に思えるかもしれないが，日本ではだめ押しはあたり前のこととされている。事前の取決め，決定ないし約束どおりに物事を円滑に運ぶためである。だめ押ししておけば，間際になって手違いの起こるおそれは少なくなる。

BANZAI

You may be startled to hear the roar of *banzai* rendered with great gusto in an airport lobby. Do not get alarmed. It is not the *banzai* attack cry of war movies, but a rousing send-off of a colleague to an overseas post.

Banzai is literally 'ten thousand years'. On the Emperor's birthday, thousands of people gather in the courtyard of the Imperial Palace to chant *banzai* (Long live the Emperor!).

Banzai is also a simple 'hurray' for felicitous occasions. Winning a baseball game, completing a building, getting elected to office or finding the answer to a puzzle – any of these call for a *banzai*. Surrounded by friends and relatives at a railway station, newly-weds are sent off on their honeymoon painfully embarrassed by the attention drawn with cries of *banzai*.

One must be there in the crowd to get the spirit of the roar of dozens of lusty male voices yelling *banzai*. Not just a cry of good wishes, it is also a group rallying cry, like the chanting of American college fraternities, boy scouts, and boisterous and drunken British rugger players. Perhaps one really should imagine the stirring cry of *banzai* as troops scramble out of the trenches to attack, to savour the rush of primeval pack instinct that *banzai* arouses.

ばんざい

　一団の日本人が空港ロビーで「ばんざい」を唱和したからといって，驚いてはいけない。第2次大戦の戦争映画に出てくる"バンザイ特攻"ではない。海外に赴任する同僚の見送りにきているのである。

　「ばんざい」を直訳すると "ten thousand years" となる。天皇誕生日に幾千もの人が皇居の庭に参集して「ばんざい」を繰り返す。このときの「ばんざい」は "Long Live the Emperor" である。

　おめでたいときの「ばんざい」は "hurrah" と同じだ。野球の試合に勝ったとき，ビルが竣工したとき，クロスワード・パズルでぴったりの単語を思いついたとき，「ばんざい」である。駅のホームで友人・親戚に囲まれて，ほやほやのカップルが新婚旅行に出かけるときも，「ばんざい」で送られる。これは，人目についてきまりの悪い「ばんざい」かもしれない。

Abura wo uru

ABURA WO URU

'What is he doing?' 'He is selling oil.' This sounds like the description of a normal activity, but in Japanese it has a derogatory meaning, implying that a person is loafing or slacking on the job. Therefore, apart from its literal meaning of 'selling oil', it can be taken to mean 'to drag one's feet', or 'to take things too easy on the job'.

In the days before electricity, street vendors went around selling rapeseed oil for lanterns. As they did not seem to be working very hard, the term *abura wo uru* became associated with 'slacking', or 'not pulling one's weight'.

Abura wo uru

油を売る

"What is he doing?" "He's selling oil" この会話の答え selling oil は立派な商売であるが, これを日本語にそのまま訳すと, ある人の仕事ぶりをそしるような意味をもつ。「油を売る」には to sell oil とは別に, loaf on the job (仕事をさぼる) の意味があるからだ。

電気がまだ発明されていなかったころ, 行商人は "あんどん" 用の油を, 通りから通りへ呼び売りして歩いたものである。彼等は仕事に精を出しているようにはみえなかった。ここから「油を売る」といえば, 現在では会社を抜け出して喫茶店で時間をつぶしているサラリーマンを指すようになった。

Apointo

APOINTO

Apointo is a corruption of the English word 'appointment'. This is an example of the way the Japanese take words from other languages and shorten them.

Although it is used in the standard sense to mean 'a prearranged meeting', it is not uncommon for a visitor with an *apointo* to be kept waiting because someone else got there before him, probably without an appointment. The fact that you just happened to be in the neighbourhood is sufficient reason to gain entry because a Japanese executive rarely refuses to see someone who drops in without an *apointo*.

In all fairness, it must be said that the new breed of Japanese businessmen are more scrupulous about keeping appointments.

Apointo

アポイント

　日本語には，外国語からの借り物で，日本の生活に合うよう，語形とか，ときには意味まで変えて使っている言葉が，たくさんある。「アポイント」は，appointment が略されたものである。

　ふつうは，面会の日時をあらかじめ取り決めておくことの意味につかう。しかしアポイントがあって訪問しても，待たされることはざらにある。前の訪問者がまだ中にいるとか，アポイントなしで訪ねた人がいることが，しょっちゅうである。「ちょっと近所まできましたので」というのが，突然訪ねるばあいの立派な理由になるからだ。日本人も日本に明るい外国のビジネスマンも，アポイントなしでやって来たからといって面会を拒まれることはめったにない。

　しかし，全体としてみると，若い世代の日本のビジネスマンは，国際感覚を身につけるようになり，アポイントメントを時間どおり，きちんと守るようになってきた。

Yakudoshi

YAKUDOSHI

One would assume that with the present high level of scientific and technical development, the Japanese would have shaken off their old-world superstitious beliefs, but this has not happened. The Japanese have held on to some of their illogical superstitions, and still retain a lot of the charm of old Japan.

Superstition still influences many things in Japanese society. One of these is *yakudoshi*. This is the belief that men and women have a predetermined unlucky age when all sorts of misfortunes are likely to befall them. During a person's unlucky period, he or she might become extraordinarily cautious and refrain from doing simple routine things.

A man's *yakudoshi* is 42 and a woman's is 33. Minor unlucky ages are 25 and 60 for men, and 19 for women.

NIPPACHI

Strictly speaking *nippachi* is not a word but a combination of two numbers: two and eight. The figures stand for the second month, February, and the eight month, August.

Weather-wise, these are the coldest months of the year in Japan, but the word has nothing to do with the weather. It is a business term that refers to the fact that February and August are traditionally the months when business is slack in Japan.

厄年

日本人が，これほどの素晴らしい技術・産業開発をとげたのは，科学する心，応用する知恵があればこそである。したがって，これほどの成果をあげた国民が，縁起をかつぐ（superstitious belief）なんて，まず誰も思うまい。ところが，さにあらず，なのである。

日本の社会には，縁起・迷信でことを決めるものがたくさんある。そのひとつが「厄年」。男女を問わず，人間には，もろもろの厄（misfortune）が一度にやってくる不幸な年回りが，前から定められているのだ，という思い込みである。この不幸な年齢になると，その人はとても用心深くなる。ふつうなら，どうということもないのに，手をつけようとしない。

男の大きな厄年は42歳，女は33歳である。小さい厄年は男25歳と60歳。女の小厄は19歳だけ。

二八（にっぱち）

厳密にいうと，にっぱちは，ちゃんとしたことばではない。ふたつの数字，2と8の組み合わせである。この数字は，1年の2番目の月と8番目の月，つまり，FebruaryとAugustからきている。

気象上からいうと，日本では2月がもっとも寒く，8月がもっとも暑い。しかし，にっぱちと気象のことは関係ない。商売用語なのである。昔から2月と8月は商売がひまな月であることをいう。

Kaki-ire-doki

'How's business?' you may ask, and if it happens to be February or August, the answer more often than not is, 'Well, you know, it's *nippachi*.' It is so universally accepted that *nippachi* is the bad time for business that it is commonly used as an acceptable excuse by people who want to put off a deal or to delay paying their bills.

KAKI-IRE-DOKI

Every year shops and department stores in Japan have two *kaki-ire-doki*: the traditional gift-giving seasons in midsummer (*ochūgen*) and December (*oseibo*). This is a term used to mean 'the seasons when earnings are good'.

Literally translated the Chinese characters for *kaki-ire-doki* mean 'the time to write in'. Some dictionaries explain it as the period when merchants are busy writing sales into their ledgers. The origin of the word, however, is not so cheerful. It meant 'put up as security' and came from recording in writing what had been put up as collateral for a loan.

Over the years the usage of the term underwent changes and eventually assumed its current meaning. The expression is not limited to describing the rush season for retailers. Other trades may have their own *kaki-ire-doki*.

「景気はどうですか？」たまたま2月か8月だったら，判で押したように，こんな答えが返ってくる。「にっぱちですからねえ」にっぱちは景気が悪い，と相場が決まっている。だから，取引を先に延ばしたいとき，支払いを待ってもらいたいとき，よく口実に使われる。にっぱちじゃ，やむを得ない，というわけだ。

書き入れ時

日本の商店やデパートでは，「書き入れ時」が年に2回ある。夏のなかばと12月で，しきたりで贈物をする季節でもある。「書き入れ時」は "the season when earnings are big"（水あげが増える時期）とか "raking-in time" の意味につかわれる。

直訳すると，time to write in である。辞書によっては「商人が売上げを元帳に書き込むのに忙しい時期」とある。しかし，元の意味は，そんなに景気のいいものではない。もとは「担保として出す」の意味で，貸付けの担保として，借用証に書き入れることからきている。

それが，いつしか使い方が変わってきて，いまのような意味になった。もちろん，このことばは，小売商の忙しい時期を指すだけとはかぎらない。他の商売にも，それぞれに書き入れ時がある。

Goshūgi

GOSHŪGI

One of the features of Japanese society is the way people observe formalities and conventions, some of which may seem irrational to the outsider. One of these is *goshūgi*. *Go* is an honorific prefix (like *o* in *ocha, ochūgen*, etc.), and *shūgi* means 'celebration' or 'congratulations'.

This is carried into the business world when one gives *goshūgi-torihiki*, or when there is a *goshūgi-sōba*. The former is a transaction made not because of its business merits but in order to express congratulations to a person or company just starting business. Literally, *goshūgi-torihiki* is 'celebration business deal'.

The latter is generally used to describe the buoyant prices on the stock exchange on the first business day of the New Year. New Year's day is a felicitous time, and it just will not do to have a slumping market, no matter what the realities are. Thus buyers and sellers usually cooperate to give the market a boost on the first day when the stock exchange reopens for business after the New Year holidays. So do not bother to look up the stock index on that day.

ご祝儀

　形式やしきたりを守ることが日本社会の特徴である。欧米の人からみると，これら形式やしきたりのなかには，不合理に思えるものもあるかもしれない。そのひとつが「ご祝儀」である。「ご」は敬語をあらわす接頭語，「祝儀」は，celebration とか congratulation の意。

　ビジネスの世界では，「ご祝儀取引」とか「ご祝儀相場」などとつかわれる。前者は商売上のうまみがあるからではなく，開業したばかりの人や企業に対するお祝いを表わすために取引することである。後者は，年明けの株式市場の大発会で，市場がにぎわうことをいう。年の始めはおめでたい時なので，現実はどうであれ，不景気なスタートを切りたくないからである。そこで買手も売手も協力して，年明けの仕事始めには，株価にはずみをつけるのである。

Gashi-kōkan

GASHI-KŌKAN

For several days after business offices reopen after the New Year holidays, businessmen are busy attending *gashi-kōkan* parties. These are functions at which people gather to exchange New Year greetings and to ask each other to treat them favourably in the new year. Most of these functions are sponsored by industrial associations, and are usually held in the daytime.

Gashi-kōkan is a very convenient function because it eliminates the need for businessmen to make time-consuming individual rounds to wish each other Happy New Year. It has a very special atmosphere because participants make determined attempts to meet as many people as possible to exchange greetings with them.

The function is also known as *meishi-kōkan*, which means 'exchanging business cards'. During the period of *gashi-kōkan* parties businessmen are excused if they are found sitting at their desks flushed with alcohol.

See MEISHI

賀詞交換

　三箇日がすぎ，仕事始めになると，数日間というもの，「賀詞交換」で忙しい。ビジネスマンが一堂に会して，新年の挨拶を交わし，「本年もどうぞよろしく」と頭を下げる。賀詞交換のパーティは，業種団体主催のばあいが多く，たいていは日中に行なわれる。

　賀詞交換会は，とても便利である。1人ずつ個別に回って，「新年おめでとう」と挨拶して歩く時間が省ける。参会者ができるだけ多くの人に挨拶しようと血眼になっているから，会場には一種独特の雰囲気がある。このパーティは「名刺交換会」ともいう。exchanging visiting card の意味である。賀詞交換会がつづいている期間は，オフィスでアルコールの匂いをプンプンさせても大目にみてもらえる。

　→ 名刺

Aisatsu-mawari

AISATSU-MAWARI

After the week-long year-end and New Year holidays, government and commercial offices reopen for business on January 4th or 5th, but the foreigner who visits a Japanese company on the first day of business expecting to discuss a deal will be frustrated.

Offices reopen, but the main business of the day is *aisatsu-mawari*, after the employees have listened to the president's traditional New Year speech in which he outlines his plans and expectations and exhorts the staff to greater endeavours in the year ahead. *Aisatsu-mawari* is 'making a round of courtesy calls'. Everyone calls on fellow employees and outside clients to say 'Happy New Year! Please continue to favour us again this year.'

The term is not limited to New Year courtesy calls but is also used for the round of calls an executive makes when he takes up a new post after having returned to Japan from an overseas posting.

挨拶まわり

　年末年始の1週間の休みが終わると、官庁や会社では、1月の4日か5日あたりから、仕事始めになる。ところが外国人がこの日に仕事をしようと思って日本の会社を訪問すると、とまどうことがよくある。

　オフィスは開いているのだが、この日の主な仕事は、まず社長恒例の年頭の辞、新年の抱負と期待、社員への激励の言葉を拝聴する。それからが「挨拶まわり」（making a round of courtesy calls）である。社内のほかの部課の人たちばかりでなく、外のお得意先にも行って「あけましておめでとうございます。今年もよろしくお願いします」（Happy New year! Please continue to favor us this year again.）と挨拶する。

　「挨拶まわり」は新年だけとは限らない。転任の役職員が着任して表敬訪問するのも、やはり「挨拶まわり」である。

On

ON

In the old days, when a feudal samurai received an *on* from a lord, he repaid the favour by offering his service, that is, his military service. In this case, the *on* was the bestowal of a fief. *On* is the act of bestowing on another person something, usually goods, which makes the receiver feel grateful and arouses in him a sense of obligation. If the thing bestowed is spiritual it is called *nasake* or *jō* (compassion). Whichever the case, this sense of obligation is *giri*.

Any act of giving which is obviously motivated by the expectation of a repayment is regarded as having been done in poor taste, or selling *on* (*on wo uru*). If one makes someone feel obligated and pushes him for repayment, it is an act of *on ni kiseru* (putting on *on*, as one puts on a garment).

When an obligation is repaid it is *on-gaeshi* (the *on* is returned). When a person neglects to repay a favour although he is able to do so, he is criticised as *on-shirazu* (ignorant of *on*). When one returns kindness with ingratitude, biting the hand that fed him, it is described as *on wo ada de kaesu* (returning *on* with vengeance). *Ada* is 'vengeance'.

Oya no on is the obligation we have towards our parents and is regarded with much gravity in Japan. *Oya no on* is mainly repaid by looking after them in their old age.

See GIRI

恩

　昔，封建武士が領主（lord）から恩を得，代わりに奉公（軍役従事）した。この場合の恩は所領（fief）である。恩は相手に感謝の念を起こし，返礼の義務感を起こさせる給付行為で，物品によることが多い。精神的なものが情（なさけ，じょう）で，いずれにしても受けた側はいつの日か返礼すべき倫理的義務，すなわち「義理」がある。

　もっとも，あからさまに返礼を期待しての恩は「恩を売る」「恩に着せる」と，かえって卑しまれる。「あなたのためにこんなことをしてあげましたよ」などというと「恩着せがましい」とそしられる。

　恩に返礼すると「恩返し」した，義理を果たしたわけで，返礼できる状態になっても知らん顔をしていると「恩知らず」と非難される。それどころか不利益な行為をするのは，「恩をアダで返す」大変な不道徳行為である。

　「親の恩」もある。生みの恩，育ての恩，これらを返すには親孝行，とくに親の晩年，その面倒をみることが大切である。もっとも最近は少々くずれてきているようだが。

　→義理

In the following pages we introduce some words which reveal styles and methods of Japanese business. These are all special commercial words, and although some have English equivalents, they carry implications that are different from the Western business world; implications that are important if one wants to study their characteristic style.

Kachō, kasei

KACHŌ, KASEI

Japanese business corporations are generally organised into divisions, departments and sections. In most cases the section is known as the *ka*. This system is known as the *kasei*.

Kasei is also used to refer to the fact that *ka* is the level at which all routine business is dealt with. The section manager, the *kachō*, therefore holds an important position in the middle management. He is the key man who leads all routine business decisions and supervises their implementation. He is normally around 40 years old.

Special project teams and groups are usually organised at the *ka* levels.

The Ministry of International Trade and Industry, MITI, however, does not adopt this terminology for most of its units. The English words 'division' and 'section' are often used.

BUCHŌ

The *buchō* is the chief of a division, reporting to the managing director, or the president of a company. Some *buchō* are members of the board of directors.

The traditional Japanese job description of the *buchō* is that he participates in intra-division meetings and chairs some intra-division meetings.

The role of the *buchō* in the big companies is similar to that of the president of a member enterprise

課長，課制

日本の会社組織は，一般に部課制をとっている。通常，section は「課」である。「課制」は section system。日常業務を処理するレベルを指すとき課制という。だから，section manager つまり「課長」は，日本では中間管理職として重要なポストにあるわけだ。年齢も40歳前後の働き盛り。日常業務をとりしきり，決定事項を監督するカナメの存在である。特別のプロジェクト・チームやグループも課レベルで組織される。

注意：通産省（MITI）では，ほとんどの課が division と呼ばれているが，まれには section と呼ばれているものもある。

部長

「部長」は chief of a division。会社の専務または社長に直属する。部長の一部は取締役である。日本では，部長職は，各部間の会議に出席したり，部内会議を主宰する。大会社の部長となると，その役割はアメリカの大コングロマリットの構成企業体の社長に匹敵するが，仕事のやり方はかなり異なる。部長が秘書に手紙を口述することはめっ

Kaigi

of a large American conglomerate, but his *modus operandi* is different.

For example, the *buchō* seldom dictates letters to his secretary. In fact, not many *buchō* have one. Instead he tells one of his subordinates what kind of letter needs to be sent out, and the draft written at a lower level comes up for the *buchō's* signature or seal through the *kakarichō* (sub-section chief) and the *kachō* (section chief).

KAIGI

It is often said that in the Japanese style of management, forming a consensus takes the place of decision-making. *Kaigi* is a meeting or conference held to discuss problems and eventually reach a consensus.

The meeting may be of members of the same department or of representatives of several departments. *Kaigi* is also a meeting with representatives of outside organisations. Some Japanese executives complain that there are too many *kaigi* in their business life, and that many such meetings could be dispensed with and be replaced instead with intra-office telephone calls, memos and the distribution of reports.

A foreign businessman calling on a Japanese executive to discuss some matter informally, should realise that he is really almost talking to the *kaigi*, because the matter will invariably be brought up at an intra-office *kaigi* afterwards.

たにない。事実，自分専属の秘書をもっている部長は，そうざらにはいない。そのかわり部長は部下に，こんな趣旨の手紙を出せ，と命ずる。手紙は下のレベルで起案され，係長（sub-section chief），課長（section chief）を経て，部長のところにあがってきて，部長の署名をもらってから出すという段取りである。

会議

日本式経営を研究している人達がよくいうが，日本では，他の国での意思決定プロセスにかわるものが，コンセンサス作りである。会議は，問題を討議し，最終的にコンセンサスに達するための a meeting または conference である。

会議に出るのは，同じ部課の人，またはいくつかの部課の代表である。会議には他社の代表との meeting もある。日本の重役は，会議が多すぎて，ろくに仕事もできない，とこぼす。電話ですませたり報告を回せば，会議を開くには及ばない，と思っている人もいる。

外国のビジネスマンが，ある問題を内々に話しあうため，日本の重役を訪問するとき，たとえ，その人には気付かれなくとも，すでに予備会議にかけられている。その問題が，あとであらためて会議にかけられるからである。

Nemawashi

Literally, *nemawashi* means 'to dig around the roots of a tree to prepare for its transplanting'. It is a key word in the business world that aptly describes the groundwork to enlist support or to secure initial consent from everyone concerned before a formal decision is made.

Japanese society operates on group decision or consensus, and *nemawashi* is an indispensable process for achieving consensus. It also avoids open confrontation. In the United States, there is a similar process known as pre-selling one's ideas, but business decisions are made regardless of whether the majority of executives are against the proposal or not.

In Japan, a proposal will be revised in the process of *nemawashi* until it is acceptable to all. So much time is spent in *nemawashi* that foreign businessmen are often exasperated waiting for a Japanese company to make a decision.

Ringi

RINGI

Ringi is the system of circulating an intra-company memorandum (the *ringi-sho*) to obtain the approval of all concerned for a course of action which may range from, say, the purchase of a word processor to the merger of two companies. Corporate decisions and plans seldom take place without a *ringi*.

Depending on the nature of the proposal, the *ringi-sho* may circulate vertically from the bottom up, or horizontally among managers and directors of related sections and divisions before coming up to the managing director or the president. It goes without saying that *nemawashi* is necessary before a *ringi-sho* is circulated. Each person puts a seal (*hanko*) of approval on it, which is the Japanese equivalent of the signature of the Western world.

The advantage of this system is that everyone becomes involved so that once a decision has been made, company-wide cooperation is assured in its implementation. Also, if anything should go wrong, responsibility is conveniently widely diffused and nobody gets blamed and loses face.

See HANKO

根回し

　本来的には、植木職人が大きな木を移植するまえに、準備として根っこの回りを掘って、太い根を切り、小さい根を出させることである。ここから転じて、正式決定に先立って、関係者に支持を求めたり、内々に同意をとりつけるため、地ならししておくことをいう。

　日本の社会は、集団の決定やコンセンサスで動く。だから「根回し」は、コンセンサス作りに欠かせぬ手順である。正面きった対決を回避することにもなる。

　アメリカでも、これに似たやり方に pre-selling（事前の売込み）というのがある。しかし、アメリカでは、全員が納得するしないにかかわりなく、決定を下してかまわない。

　日本では、ある案件について、根回ししてゆくうちに、修正を加えて、全員に受け入れられるような方式のものにする。だから根回しには時間がかかる。外国のビジネスマンは、日本の会社でなかなか決定が出ないため、しびれを切らしてしまうことがよくある。

稟議（りんぎ）

「稟議」とは，小はワードプロセッサーの購入から，大は会社の合併に至るまで，予定案件について，関係者全員の承諾をとりつけるため，部内に文書（稟議書）を回付する仕組みをいう。会社の意思決定なり措置が，なんらかの稟議抜きで行なわれることはまずない。

提案の内容によって，稟議には，下から上にあがってゆくタテ型と，関係部課長の間に回されるヨコ型があり，最後には，事と次第によって専務なり社長のところへゆく。稟議書が回される前に根回しを十分にしておくことが大切である。関係者は承認したしるしに，それぞれ印鑑を押す。印鑑は欧米の署名と同じである。

稟議制のいいところは，みんなが関与しているので，いったん決定が下されると，その実行に会社全体が協力する。うまくいかなかった場合でも，みんなの責任になるので，特定の人が傷つくことはない。

　→はんこ

Negai, todoke

NEGAI, TODOKE

Negai, meaning 'request', and *todoke*, meaning 'report', are forms of paperwork which keep the administration of large Japanese companies flowing smoothly.

Prescribed *negai* and *todoke* forms have to be filled in for routine matters such as requests for leave, office supply payments, change of employee's address, changes in employee's family composition, etc.

The *negai* and *todoke* systems are also used in submissions or reports or notifications to government offices, concerning both business and private matters. The paperwork, though indeed troublesome, is essential to administrative efficiency.

See JIHYŌ

Negai, todoke

願い，届け

「願い」は request,「届け」は report である。この書式がないと，大きな会社は順調に機能しない。

願いと届けは，あらかじめ書式ができていて，日常きまりきった事項について，書き込めばよいだけになっている。願いには，休暇願い（年次休暇，病気欠勤，出産休暇など）や事務用品請求の願いなど。届けには，住所変更届け，家族異動届け（出産，死亡など），作業変更届けなどがある。

仕事上ないし個人的な事柄について，官公庁に要請やら報告もしくは通告するときにも，書式による願いや届けを提出する。書類を書くことは，面倒なようにもみえるが，これがないことには，事務効率がさっぱり上がらないのである。

→辞表

Soko wo nantoka
SOKO WO NANTOKA

A businessman sometimes finds himself caught in difficult negotiations. The more he listens to the other side's explanations and arguments, the more hopeless his own case seems to become. The face of his boss appears before his eyes and he realises that he cannot go back to him with the conditions laid down by the other side.

At such a time, the words that come out of his mouth are '*soko wo nantoka* . . .'. *Soko* means 'that' and in this case it is a reference to the stated position, conditions or contention of the other party. *Nantoka* is a vague way of saying 'please ease or moderate your conditions' or 'please accept even a small part of our conditions'. It carries the meaning of 'please be a little more conciliatory so that we could somehow find a way to reach agreement'.

Greater stress is put into the appeal by inserting the word *magete* (bend) – *soko wo magete nantoka* . . .

This is an expression which is often used by Japanese businessmen because they generally do not like to be restricted to inflexible, rational Western management style of negotiations.

Soko wo nantoka

そこをなんとか

　むずかしい交渉ごとにいやいやながらも出かけていく。相手の説明を聞けば聞くほど、絶望的になってくる。だが、そのときチラリと浮かぶのがコワイ上司の顔……。こんな条件では絶対にウンとはいってくれない。思わず「そこをなんとか」といいたくなる。

　この場合、「そこ」とは相手の立場、示されている条件など意味しているが、「なんとか」とは「お願いします、条件を和らげてください」「当方の条件を一部でもお引き受け下さい」といった程度で、「なんとか」とは双方の合意点に達する何らかの方法・手段を見つけたいぐらいの意味が込められている。

　かならずしもビジネスライクな交渉をよしとしない日本の社会では、しばしば使われる言葉である。もっと強調する場合には「そこを曲げてなんとか」という。「神様、仏様、～様」と拝み倒さんばかりの頼み方もあるが、これは少々オーバーであろう。

Hanko

HANKO

Without this little piece of ivory or bone, slightly thicker than a pencil and about five centimetres long, business in Japan would quickly come to a standstill. The *hanko*, the personal seal, is like the Westerner's personal signature.

Most corporate decisions must await the completion of the process whereby documents are read and approved and then stamped with the *hanko* by all concerned. This process rarely results in hasty decisions. The seal businessmen use in signing routine papers is usually a *san·mon-ban*, which is readily available at stationery stores.

Hanko is shortened to *han* and is pronounced *ban* when used in combination with other words, such as *san·mon-ban*.

See RINGI

はんこ

鉛筆よりやや太目，長さ5センチほどのこの道具がないことには，日本で商売はたちどころに行き詰まってしまう。「はんこ」つまり seal が署名代わりにつかわれる。

たいていの企業の決定は，文書を読み，承認し，それから関係者全員がはんこをつくまでは，完了しない。この手続きのために，早急な決定はしにくい。ビジネスマンがきまりきった書類に押すときに使う印鑑は，たいていは三文判。出来あいで，文具店で買える代物である。

「はんこ」は短くして「はん」(判) という。「三文判」のように，他の言葉と組み合わせたとき，「ばん」と発音することがある。

→稟議

Meishi

MEISHI

The *meishi* (calling card) is another item like the *hanko* (the personal seal) that appears quite necessary to Japanese businessmen. When two people meet for the first time, the *meishi* are exchanged after all the bowing or hand-shaking. Any businessman who cannot produce a *meishi* will be at a disadvantage. Businessmen keep a file of all the cards they collect, which is referred to when the time comes to send out seasonal greeting cards.

Many Japanese businessmen have bilingual *meishi* with their name, position, company name, address, telephone and telex numbers in Japanese on one side and in English on the other. If foreign businessmen visiting Japan want to be remembered, they should have their *meishi* printed in the same manner. In most large hotel arcades, there are shops which will print *meishi* within 24 hours.

One should note that the Japanese these days usually rearrange their names to conform to the Western pattern with the surname or family name last, preceded by the personal name.

名刺

　「名刺」(calling card or name card)は，日本では，社交とくに仕事の接触には欠せない。初対面では，欧米のように握手をしないで，名刺を交換する。名刺を出せない人は，最初の印象を損なう。

　ビジネスマンは，名刺のファイルを作っておく。クリスマスカードや年賀状を出す季節になると役に立つ。

　日本のビジネスマンの名刺には，氏名，肩書，会社名，住所，電話番号が，片面ずつ日本語と英語で記されている。

　訪日する外国のビジネスマンが末永く覚えておいてもらいたいと思ったら，日本式の名刺を作ることである。主なホテルのアーケードには，24時間で名刺を作ってくれる店がある。

Personnel matters

This next section brings us to the level of the Japanese organisational set-up, drawing special attention to personnel matters: the finer points of the basic employment system, recruitment and resignation, company motto, part-time work, annual leave, salary, are individually elaborated upon.

SHŪSHIN-KOYŌ

Much has been written and said about the advantages, to both the company and the employee, of the Japanese lifetime employment system (*shūshin-koyō*). Although the system offers security to the worker, it also makes it extremely difficult for a person to change his job.

For the individual, it is therefore vital to join a good company after graduation. For management, it is vital to secure qualified personnel who will stay with the company for the next 35 years or so. This means that the competition to recruit new staff and the competition among new graduates or school-leavers to get the best jobs, is very severe.

The era of low growth of the Japanese economy has begun to expose the drawbacks of the *shūshin-koyō*. Companies having to retain old employees whose salaries are high but whose contributions have declined are feeling the disadvantages of the system. Thus *kibō-taishoku*, encouraging voluntary early retirement, is growing.

See KIBŌ-TAISHOKU, SHUKKŌ-SHAIN

Shūshin-koyō

終身雇用

　日本の「終身雇用」制度(lifetime employment system)は、会社にとっても従業員にとっても、雇用の安定を保証してくれる。しかし、同時に、中途で会社を変えにくい。

　その人にとって、学校卒業と同時に良い会社に入るのは、きわめて重要である。会社にとっても、この先35年くらい働いてもらうのだから、役に立つ有能な人材を確保するのはきわめて重要である。それだけに、入社試験を受け、採用になるのは、厳しい競争ということになる。

　低成長時代とともに、終身雇用制の欠陥が目につきはじめてきた。会社としては、給料が高い割に有用度の落ちてきている高年齢者を抱えておかねばならないとあって、痛手を感じるようになった。そこで導入されるのが、希望退職制度である。

Kibō-taishoku

KIBŌ-TAISHOKU

Under the lifetime employment system, there is a compulsory retirement age which generally ranges between 55 and 60. The retiring employee automatically receives a retirement allowance calculated according to a ratio indexed to his length of service and basic salary. However, sometimes an employee does resign of his own accord. This is known as *jiko-taishoku*. If an employee resigns for personal reasons before his automatic retirement age, the allowance will be considerably reduced.

When the *oil-shokku* (the oil crisis of 1973) reduced corporation earnings, many companies trimmed down and cut overheads. Instead of dismissing employees outright, some individuals were offered early retirement, with benefits considerably more than the standard. Employees who took advantage of this offer were treated as *kibō-taishoku*, differentiating them from those who resigned of their own accord (*jiko-taishoku*). Literally, *kibō-taishoku* is 'retiring with hopes'.

See JIHYŌ, KATA-TATAKI

Kibō-taishoku

希望退職

日本は終身雇用制であり，どの会社にも定年がある。いまは，大体55歳から60歳の間である。退職者には自動的に退職金が支給される。勤続年数と基本給を基準に一定の割合を掛けた額である。定年まえに個人的な理由で退職するばあい，退職金は標準よりずっと少なくなる。

石油価格の急騰で，会社が減益になったため，経費切詰めの"減量"政策をとるところが多かった。たとえば，100人をすっはり解雇する代わりに，標準額よりもかなりの色をつけて自発的退職を求める。この申し出に乗る人は，「希望退職」扱いとなる。自分の意思でやめることには変わりないのだが，個人的な理由による「自己退職」とは違う。

→ 辞表，肩たたき

CHŌREI

At many Japanese factories and offices, the working day begins with *chōrei*. This traditional institution, a source of amazement to Westerners, is something like a morning pep talk.

In some companies, the president gives a brief talk. In large companies, each section holds its own *chōrei*, with the section manager giving the pep talk. At some offices, the workers go through a set of limbering-up exercises and finish off by singing the company song or shouting the company slogan, or reciting the *shaze* (company motto or objective) in unison.

The meeting lasts only a few minutes, but it helps create a 'let's go' mood and a feeling of identity with the group. *Chōrei* is usually held every morning, but some companies schedule it only on the first day of the week.

SHAZE, SHAKUN

Most Japanese companies have either a *shaze* or a *shakun* or both. *Sha* means company. *Ze* means precept. *Shaze* therefore means a statement of corporate principles and ideals, and loosely corresponds to the motto of a Western corporation. *Shakun* is a statement of basic precepts or exhortations directed at company employees.

朝礼

　日本の工場や職場では、朝礼とともに1日の仕事を始めるところが多い。この昔からの制度（欧米の人にはなんとも奇妙に映る）は一種の morning pep talk である。会社によっては、社長みずから短い訓話をする。大会社では、部課ごとに朝礼をやり、部課長が激励の訓辞をする。職場によっては、軽い体操などもやり、締めくくりに社歌の合唱や会社の信条を唱和する。朝礼は2、3分程度で終わるが、"やる気"を起こさせ、一体感を生み出す。朝礼は毎朝行なうのがふつうだが、週の初日だけやるところもある。これは"月曜の朝の憂鬱病"（Monday morning blues）を吹き飛ばす効果がある。

社是, 社訓

　日本の会社は、たいてい社是とか社訓、またはその両方をもっている。「社」は company。「是」は what is right とか justification（正しいこと）。「訓」は precept（戒律）。ここから「社是」とは会社の原則や理想を宣明したもの。欧米の企業の「モットー」と思えばよい。「社訓」は従業員にたいする基本的な教えとか勧めを述べたもの。

Seifuku

Shaze is usually tersely expressed in lofty, high-sounding, formalised language. *Shakun* sometimes takes the same form but is more often couched in ordinary language.

The original is usually written in brush calligraphy, framed and hung up in the president's office or the boardroom.

Shaka is the company song.

SEIFUKU

Tellers, typists, secretaries and all other female employees of banks work in company uniforms: *seifuku*. So do girls at securities and insurance companies, department stores and supermarkets. Almost all girls working in large Japanese companies wear uniforms either in offices or factories.

Nearly all the top companies provide uniforms for women, but only a few provide uniforms for white-collar male workers. Men often wear company badges on their suit lapels.

Japanese regard the uniform as an important part of the company image and more and more companies are using top designers like Hanae Mori to design their uniforms.

「社是」は簡潔高尚で仰々しく,いかめしいことばづかいであることが多い。だが「社訓」は,これに似ているが,もっと分かりやすいことばになっているばあいが多い。

そもそもは墨筆で書かれ,額に入れて社長室や会議室に掲げられていた。会社によっては,毎朝の仕事始めに従業員が唱和するしきたりのところがある。

制服

銀行では,窓口係,タイピスト,秘書など女子行員は,お仕着せのユニホーム「制服」を着る。証券会社や保険会社,デパート,スーパーでも同じだ。大会社に勤める女性も,ほとんど全員が,オフィスでも工場でも,お揃いのユニホームである。

トップの企業2000社のうち,女性に制服を支給していないところは,ほんの僅かしかない。逆に男子の事務職に制服を着せている会社もめったにない。代わりに男子は,上衣の襟の折返しに会社のバッジを付けている所が多い。

会社の制服は,その企業イメージにつながるところ大とあって,森英恵などの国際的に有名なデザイナーに頼む会社がふえてきて,ギャルたちにも喜ばれている。

JIREI

Jirei is a piece of paper that brings joy or dismay to employees of private companies or government servants. Usually just a couple of lines on a single sheet of paper, the *jirei* notifies an individual that he has been employed, transferred, reassigned, dismissed or retired. The *jirei* is worded as an order. No personnel changes are carried out without a *jirei*.

Spring is the season of the *jirei* because it is the time when recruits fresh out of college are taken in *en masse* and companies make a wholesale reshuffle of assignments. Once a *jirei* is issued there is no chance of it being withdrawn.

There is, however, one type of *jirei* which is not final. This is the *shimbun jirei* (newspaper *jirei*), the name given cynically to newspaper reports of pending appointments of top-level officers.

JINJI-IDŌ

March is a month of anxious expectation for workers in the Japanese corporate world because of the large-scale staff re-deployments carried out at this time. This is *jinji-idō*, the movement of people which is done before the new fiscal year begins. A smaller change is sometimes made in October.

Periodic job rotation of personnel at all levels is a common practice in Japan. It is accepted as a system for developing human resources and grooming a versatile managerial class which has a company-wide outlook.

辞令

「辞令」は，会社や官庁に働く日本人にとって，哀歓をわける一片の紙である。ふつう「辞令」は1枚の紙にわずか2，3行で書かれた採用，昇進，降等，異動，配転，解雇，退職などの伝達書である。一般に，その語調は命令調で，これなしに人事異動は行なわれない。

春は辞令の季節である。大学を出たばかりの新人が大量に採用されるし，組織全体が大幅な異動を行なう時期だからだ。いったん辞令が出てしまうと，撤回されることはない。辞令には，本決まりでないものもある。これを「新聞（ newspaper ）辞令」という。新聞がトップ・レベルの人事を未決定のうちに報道してしまうのを皮肉ったいい方である。

人事異動

3月は，日本の会社に働く人にとって，不安と期待の交錯する月である。会社も官庁も，4月の新年度を機会に，年に1度の大規模な「人事異動」(staff reassignment)を行なうからである（小異動が10月ごろにある）。どのレベルでも，定期的に仕事が変わるのは，日本では通例である。これは人的能力を開発する仕組みである。いろいろな仕事をなんでもこなし，全社的な視野から物がみられる管理職の人材を育成しよう，というものである。

Arubaito

At the middle management level, certain posts are considered stepping stones to top-level promotion. Thus, under the Japanese seniority system, people who reach an age that qualify them for key posts are particularly anxious in spring because the next *jinji-idō* may determine the rest of their career in the company. *Jinji-idō* is an important event for outsiders too, because it directly affects their contacts in the company.

See JIREI

ARUBAITO

Arubaito is a distortion of the German word *arbeit* which means 'work'. The Japanese have taken hundreds of words from other languages and rewritten them in a form that they can pronounce. This often distorts their sounds beyond recognition in the original language. And in many cases the meaning of the word is changed quite drastically from the original. *Arubaito* is one of these.

Today *arubaito* refers to part-time work or temporary work or moonlighting. Students who work to earn pocket money or to pay for their fees are doing *arubaito*.

Companies often carry a category of workers called *arubaito* who work regular hours but are treated differently from regular employees. They are paid by the hour or by the day and are not given any of the substantial fringe benefits that regular employees receive. Piecework *arubaito* is usually done at home.

See NAISHOKU

Arubaito

　中間管理職には，重役への階段と目されるポストがいくつかある。したがって，年功序列制の日本では，重要なポストにそろそろ就いてもいい年齢に達した人は，とりわけ気がもめる。次の人事異動次第で，これからどこまで昇進できるかが決まってしまうからだ。人事異動は，社外の人にも重要である。その会社とのつながりに直接影響が出てくるからである。

アルバイト

　「アルバイト」は，もともと日本語ではない。ドイツ語のArbeit（労働の意）が日本語化した言葉である。本来の意味から変わって日本的なものになっている外国語は何千とある。

　このように「アルバイト」は，パートタイムや一時的な仕事などのことをいう。小遣いや学資をかせぐため，学生は「アルバイト」をする。

　会社もアルバイトと称する部類の人を雇うことがよくある。正規の時間どおり働いても，正社員と待遇の違う人達である。賃金は時給ないし日給で，正社員と違って賃金外の諸手当は支給されない。出来高払い制のアルバイトは，家ですることが多い。

NAISHOKU

In the old feudal days, *naishoku* meant the side-jobs of the samurai or the *rōnin*, the wandering samurai. Though the samurai's main task was to fight for his master, he often supplemented his earnings by doing something on the side. Today, it generally means the manual piecework which a housewife does at home. The number of housewives who work outside the home in part-time jobs or as cosmetics or life insurance salespersons has increased recently, but this type of work is not called *naishoku*. Such work is known as *arubaito*. Literally, *naishoku* is 'inside work' or 'an inside occupation'.

When a married woman holds a permanent job it is known either as *tomo-bataraki* (working together) or *tomo-kasegi* (earning together). *Naishoku* is only used for work at home.

When an employee takes work home from the office, he might say jokingly to his friends, 'I am going to do *naishoku* tonight,' although he will not get any payment for it. The fact that he is going to do it at home allows the use of *naishoku*.

If you spend your weekends at home writing a novel, you are doing *naishoku*. If you spend your weekends at home making furniture as a hobby, you will not be doing *naishoku*. The Sunday artist or the Sunday carpenter pursuing a hobby does not do *naishoku*.

See ARUBAITO

内職

　古くは武士の副職，浪人の仕事として行なわれたものを指したが，現在では，一般に主婦が家内で行なう手作業的賃仕事を指すようになった。もっとも最近では主婦がパート・タイマーや化粧品のセールスマン，保険外交員など家庭外に出て働くことが多くなったが，これはアルバイトと呼ばれ，内職とはいわない。また主婦が結婚以前から，あるいは結婚後でも恒常的に仕事をもっているばあいは共働きとか共稼ぎといって区別する。あくまで家内で行なう仕事が内職と呼ばれる。

　会社の仕事を一部家にもって帰って片付けるばあいも別に手当がもらえるわけではないが「今晩内職するよ」と冗談でいったりすることもある。近頃，週末を利用して小説を書いたりする人も多いが，これは内職のひとつである。
── ただし趣味的なものは日曜大工とか日曜画家といって，内職に大工をしているとはいわない。

Shukkō-shain

SHUKKŌ-SHAIN

In Japan, the mobility of white-collar workers is very low. People normally stay with the same company till their retirement. Thus a Japanese company does not have the advantage of being able to take in a man with a different experience, as Western companies can. And so in Japan employees are sometimes seconded to other companies temporarily. Such an employee is called a *shukkō-shain*.

The *shukkō-shain* normally works on a loan basis, with the understanding that he will be given the chance to return to his original company. However, some people choose to stay with the new company for the rest of their lives.

Senior executives are loaned to subsidiaries to assist the subsidiary. Banks loan executives to companies they finance. Manufacturers loan sales engineers to distributors. Central government agencies loan officials to local government organisations and to trade and industry associations. The system not only brings the organisations which are involved in the temporary exchange closer together, but also gives the employees concerned a chance to see another side of the business world, and thus compensates for the immobility of white-collar workers.

Shukkō-shain

出向社員

　日本では，事務系統の人が会社を変わることはめったにない。ある会社に入ると，ふつうは定年までそこで働くつもりでいる。しかし，会社側がある従業員を一時ほかの会社勤務に回すことがある。回された従業員を「出向社員」という。

　ふつうはもとの会社に戻すという約束で貸し出すわけだが，そのまま最後まで新しい会社に居残る人もいる。

　専任重役でも，子会社強化のために出向する。銀行は，融資先の会社に，経理担当として重役を出向させる。製造会社は，流通部門に，販売の専門家を出向させる。中央政府機関は，地方自治体や業界団体に，役人を出向させる。

　出向社員制度は，一種の管理職スカウトみたいなものだが，他の国では珍しいことではない。

Teate

TEATE

The monthly salary of most Japanese corporate employees consists of two parts – apart from the so-called basic pay there are the various allowances which are called *teate*. There are dozens of different types of *teate*.

Some are based on the individual's personal situation (allowances for dependents, housing allowances, etc.). Some are pegged to the job (responsibility allowance for managers, special allowance for being able to operate a certain machine, overtime, night-work allowance, etc.).

This system makes it seem that the *teate* is something extra and additional to one's regular pay. In practice both employer and employee take *teate* as part of the total monthly payment. The present general trend is to discontinue this breaking down of the employees' remuneration into so many different allowances, and they are being lumped together into one single pay-packet in more and more companies.

手当

　日本の会社員の月給は、たいてい2本立てである。いわゆる本俸、それに「手当」と称するもろもろの賃金外給与である。手当の項目を並べたら、このページがらくに一杯になるほど、たくさんある。

　その人の個人的状況から割り出されるもの（扶養家族手当、住宅手当など）、仕事内容と結びついたもの（役職手当、特殊機器操作手当、過勤手当、夜勤手当など）がある。

　この仕組みからわかるように、「手当」とは、決まった給料とは別建てのものをいう。しかし、実際には従業員も会社側も、手当を月給の一部とみなしている。その証拠に、本俸と手当を別にわけて支給する習慣はなく、月給として、込みで払うようになってきている。

Tenbiki

TENBIKI

It is rare for the Japanese employee to receive his full salary each month. Under the *tenbiki* system a great many deductions are made. In accordance with the law, income tax is withheld at source, as are payments for health, unemployment insurance and social security. Unions also make agreements to collect union dues direct from pay-packets.

Other deductions made are for supplies to the employees from the company. (These are for goods and services bought through the company, saving schemes contributions, insurance premiums, rents for company housing, etc.)

Although these *tenbiki* reduce the take-home pay considerably, there does not seem to be any dissatisfaction with the system.

BŌNASU

Japanese salaried workers receive bonuses twice a year, normally in June/July and December. *Bōnasu* is derived from the English word 'bonus', and given a typical Japanese twist in the pronunciation to cope with the 's' sound. The *bōnasu* is between one to three months' salary.

天引き

　日本の会社員は,「天引き」制度があるので,毎月の給料を額面どおりにまるまる支給されることはない。法律によって,所得税が源泉徴収される。健康保険,失業保険,社会保障などの払込金も差し引かれる。会社と労組との合意により組合費も給料差引きである。

　さらに,会社と社員と物品・サービス納入業者との三者取決めで引かれる分がある。会社を通して買った商品の月賦代金,積立貯金,グループ保険の払込金など,まだある。社宅の家賃など,会社の規定にもとづく差引分がある。

　こうしたもろもろの「天引き」で,月給袋は軽くなるばかりだが,便利でもあるので,社員から苦情は出ない。

ボーナス

　日本のサラリーマンは,年に2回,ふつうは6/7月と12月に「ボーナス」の形で一時金をもらう。その額は,平均して月給の1カ月分から3カ月分である。

Bōnasu

The *bōnasu* started as a profit-sharing system. Before World War II, the management of a company which had done well in the six months preceding the bonus paid out large bonuses: up to six months' salary, or even more. In bad times the bonus was small, or even not paid at all.

Today, workers regard the bonus as an integral part of their annual salary. They cover their day-to-day expenses with their monthly pay and use the bonus for buying special items like expensive clothes, cookers, television sets. A good part of the *bōnasu* is put away for future expenses such as children's education. This is one good reason why the Japanese savings rate is so high. Labour unions claim that the bonus is a form of deferred payment and is the employees' rightful entitlement, and there have been strikes on the amount of bonus.

Many Japanese companies pay staff salaries into their bank accounts, which in effect put the money into the hands of their wives, but the *bōnasu* is usually handed to the employee directly, thus giving him a chance to take a slice off for himself before bringing it home.

Bōnasu

「ボーナス」は，そもそもは利益金分配制度であった。第2次大戦前は，会社の過去6カ月の業績が良いと，経営側は多額のボーナスを支給した（ときにはサラリーの6カ月以上ということさえあった）。業績不振だと，ボーナスはすずめの涙ほどかゼロであった。

ところが今日では「ボーナス」は給与の不可分の一部だ，と労働者はみなしている。日常の支払いは月給ですませ，高価な衣服とか耐久財をボーナスで買うのである。ボーナスのかなりの部分は，子供の教育費といった将来の出費に備えて貯金する。これが，日本人の貯蓄率の高い理由のひとつとなっている。労組は，ボーナスを一種の後払い賃金とみなしており，労働者の当然の権利だとする。ボーナス支給額をめぐってストライキをすることも珍しくない。

Shain-ryō

SHAIN-RYŌ

Large Japanese companies maintain dormitories called *shain-ryō* for their employees. Multi-storied dormitories for bachelors whose families live outside the city are known as *tanshin-ryō*.

Companies which have many branches in various cities throughout the country maintain dormitories in each city for employees transferred from another city.

The use of these dormitories is voluntary and there are different company rules and regulations to determine who may occupy them. The communal dormitory life helps to generate a strong camaraderie among staff. Fees are usually nominal.

Some companies provide housing for families, which is known as *sha-taku* (company housing).

KAKI-KYŪKA

Kaki-kyūka means 'summer vacation'. Although it is not on the scale of the European countries, *kaki-kyūka* has become in recent years an established institution in Japan. It is customary for an entire factory to shut down for a week or thereabouts during the hottest part of summer, while office staff draw up rosters to take their summer vacation in turns. Many companies encourage their staff to take their annual leave in July or August in addition to the special *kaki-kyūka*.

社員寮，単身寮

　日本の大会社は，従業員用に「社員寮」という寄宿舎を設備している。家族を遠くに残してひとりで赴任してきている従業員用の宿舎が「単身寮」である。

　全国あちこちの都市に，大きな支店なり，施設のあるところでは，寮があって，他の地域から転勤してきた従業員の宿舎にあてている。

　寮に入る，入らないは，自由であるが，ひとつ屋根の下に寝起きすれば，連帯意識が生まれる。寮費は，あまり高くはなく，月給から天引きされる。

　企業によっては，家族用の一戸建て住宅を提供するところもある。これを「社宅」という。

夏季休暇

　「夏季休暇」とは summer vacation のこと。欧米並みとまではいかないが，日本でも近年は夏季休暇が定着してきた。夏の暑い盛りに，工場全体が1週間くらい閉まるのは，当たり前になってきた。事務職も予定をやりくりして交代で休暇をとる。年次休暇も夏季休暇に加えて，7月と8月にとるよう勧めている会社も多い。会社員は夏休みに

Yūkyū-kyūka

The businessman uses the summer vacation to make up for the time he has spent away from his family, and takes them to the seaside or to the mountains, getting away from the intense Japanese summer heat and the bustle of the cities.

See YŪKYŪ-KYŪKA

YŪKYŪ-KYŪKA

This is paid leave. Salaried workers in Japan are given about twenty days paid leave in addition to Sundays, twelve national holidays, and if their company is on a five-day week, Saturdays.

The number of paid holidays depends on the length of service. Generally, it starts with seven days for the first year, and increases by two days each year up to a maximum of twenty.

The older generation, particularly white-collared businessmen, do not take all their *yūkyū-kyūka* because they say they are too busy. The younger generation takes paid vacations for granted, and their lifestyle is gradually influencing the older corporate employees.

海や山に出かけて，家族を楽しませ，日本のむし暑い夏をしのごうとする。

有給休暇

　給料が支払われる休暇（the paid leave）のこと。日本のサラリーマンには，年に20日間くらいの「有給休暇」（paid holidays）がある。もちろん，日曜，祝祭日12日，それに週5日制のところでは土曜も有給の休日に加えられる。

　有給休暇の日数は，勤続年数（length of service）による。1年目が年7日，あと年2日ずつふえて，最高20日間といったところだ。

Seiri-kyūka

It has now become customary for most salaried workers to take a week-long vacation in summer, if they can fit it in with their workloads.

See KAKI-KYŪKA

SEIRI-KYŪKA

This is a special leave for women workers during their menstrual period stipulated by the labour laws. It is an interesting case of consideration for the discomfort of a group, contrary to the prevailing social position of women, and at the expense of productivity.

A standing joke in the business world is that employees who are sent to another city and who are given special leave to return home to their families now and then, are granted a male version of *seiri-kyūka*.

年輩の人，とりわけ事務職のビジネスマンは，せっかく有給休暇がありながら，こなそうとしないばあいが多い。忙しくて休んでなんかいられない，というのが口ぐせだ。若い世代になると，有給休暇は当たり前のこととして，がっちり休む。その生活態度に年輩組も感化されるようになってきた。

いまでは，サラリーマンだと夏に1週間の休暇をとるのはざらである。もっとも，仕事のやりくりをつけて，それだけ休めれば，の話だが。

生理休暇

労働基準法に定められた女性だけに請求権のある月一回の休暇である。有給休暇とは別で，女性の生理に伴う苦痛に労働の負担を上乗せするのはかわいそうだとの法律上の配慮である。もっとも苦痛には個人差があり，職種によっても労働負担が異なるから，この休暇制度は不公平との声もある。

ところが，生理休暇は男性もとる。月に1度か2度，「単身赴任」社員が下着などの汚れ物を詰めた大きな鞄を持って家族の待つわが家に帰る休暇のことを，からかい気味に生理休暇と呼んでいるのだ。

会社によっては2／3カ月に1度，単身赴任社員の自宅に近い事務所や支店に社用出張をさせることもある。社員福祉の一方法であろうが，この場合生理出張とは呼ばないようだ。

TEIKI-SAIYŌ, CHŪTO-SAIYŌ

Japanese corporations make it a practice to recruit workers regularly once a year in spring, the time when students graduate from high schools and universities. This annual hiring is called *teiki-saiyō*. The big corporations take in hundreds of graduates at a time.

The recruitment is not necessarily based on the need to fill a vacancy or to employ people to do a specific job. The number of people they hire is determined by the company's long-term strategic policy: another example of the far-sighted approach that characterises Japanese business.

If a company should find it necessary to hire people outside the *teiki-saiyō* process, the form adopted is called the *chūto-saiyō* (mid-stream hiring). This may occur when a person with specialised skills or knowledge is suddenly needed or when a company expands its operations and needs a large number of people at once.

Teiki-saiyō, chūto-saiyō

定期採用, 中途採用

日本の会社は, 年に一度, 高校・大学卒業期の春に社員採用するのがしきたりである。この採用を「定期採用」という。大会社ともなると, 何百人もの新卒をとる。

採用はかならずしも空きを埋める必要があるからとか, 特定の仕事につける人達を雇うため, とはかぎらない。何名採用するかは, それぞれの会社の長期の戦略的考慮から割り出される。

会社が, 定期採用の枠外で雇い入れる必要が生じたとき, 「中途採用」する。特殊技能者を急に入用とするときとか, 会社の事業拡大で経験ある人材を一度に大量に必要とするとき, 中途採用が行なわれる。

Shin·nyū-shain

SHIN·NYŪ·SHAIN

The Japanese academic year starts on the first of April. University entrance examinations are held in early March. Final year examinations take place at the end of February or in early March. These examination pressures on students result in a delayed reaction in May. Suicides are not uncommon at this time. They have a word for this period: *gogatsu-byō* (May sickness). In April the new crop of high-school and university graduates are taken into the corporate fold. Although graduation is in the spring, the recruits known as *shin·nyū-shain* are almost all chosen by the end of the preceding year by the *aota-gai* process.

Every company holds a formal ceremony to welcome the recruits, with the president giving a speech telling them what is expected of them and what they can expect of the company during their lifetime employment. It is a major moment in the lives of these young men and the occasion is treated with the gravity it deserves.

They are then given a basic training course during which the company spirit is hammered into them. This training may last between a week to a couple of months. In some cases they go to a company retreat where they eat and sleep together to cement *dōki* (same time) ties. After the induction training period, they are assigned to their various sections for on-the-job training of the special skills of their specific duties.

See AOTA-GAI

Shin·nyū-shain

新入社員

　4月は，どの会社もほやほやの高卒や大卒を社員に迎える月である。卒業は春だが，「新入社員」は，青田買いで前の年の終わりまでにほとんど全員が採用内定ずみになっている。

　どの会社も新入社員歓迎式を行ない，社長が訓示する。これからの会社生活で，会社は社員になにを期待するか，会社から何が期待できるか，を説く。

　新入社員は，このあと研修を受ける。この期間に会社の精神を叩き込まれ，会社の事業のあらましを頭に入れる。この研修は，会社によって1週間ないし数カ月もつづく。ときには会社の休養施設に"缶詰"にし，寝食をともにしながら同期の連帯感を固める。研修期間が終わると，各課に配属されて実地訓練を受け，仕事を身につける。

Aota-gai

AOTA-GAI

Aota-gai is a phrase that comes from the farms. Today it is hardly ever heard in the rural communities but it has become an indispensable phrase in personnel management.

In the old days, it meant 'buying rice on the stalk' before it was harvested. It is similar to buying beef on the hoof, or wool on the sheep's back. Poor farmers in need of cash received advances from merchants in exchange for a promise to deliver the rice when it was harvested.

Aota-gai (literally 'to buy a green padi field') is used today to describe the raiding of schools to sign up prospective employees from the students who are about to graduate. The phrase *aota-gari* is sometimes used instead of *aota-gai*. This means 'cutting green padi', which suggests a more aggressive attack on the young helpless students. Slashing the green and unripe also conveys some of the critical undertones to this intensive competitive recruitment drive.

See SHIN-NYŪ-SHAIN

青田買い

「青田買い」は、もともと農業用語であった。今日では、農業用語としてつかわれるのはごくまれで、企業社会に欠かせない用語のひとつになっている。昔は、刈入れまえに buying rice on the stalk の意味だった。牛肉を生きた牛のまま買い予約するとか、羊毛を羊から刈るまえに買い予約するのと同じである。貧しい農家が、現金をどうしても必要なとき、穫れたお米で返す約束で、商人から前借りすることである。

「青田買い」(直訳すると、to buy a green paddy field)は、企業が学校にアタックをかけて、翌春卒業見込みの学生から入社の約束をとりつけることをいう。「青田買い」のかわりに「青田刈り」(to reap the green paddy field)ということもある。企業が、新入社員の獲得に早いうちから一所懸命に奔走するさまをいう。

Informal channels of communication

In the Japanese style of personnel management, concerted formal efforts are constantly made to weld a company into a cohesive homogeneous whole, an example being that of the *chōrei*, the morning pep talk before the working day begins. Paralleling this, however, is a warmer, more personal channel of communication quietly carried out to iron out conflicts of individuals and the group. Managers create opportunities to talk to their men alone or in small groups, and often interact with them on an informal social basis. The phrases that follow indicate how some of this subtle smoothening takes place.

OCHA WO NOMU

Probably no other people drink tea (*ocha wo nomu*) during office hours as much as the Japanese. The first thing workers do when they get to the office in the morning is to drink green tea. Tea is served again at mid-morning and at mid-afternoon. As soon as a visitor is seated, he is served green tea. Tea is served at all business meetings.

Very frequently, co-workers go out during office hours to a neighbourhood coffee shop to *ocha wo nomu*. The phrase can also refer to drinking coffee. The purpose usually is a tête-a-tête. So, when a fellow worker asks, 'Won't you come and have a cuppa with me?' he is in fact saying, 'Let's have a quiet chat.' And the chat is usually about personnel matters. Very often, drinking tea together is also used as an opportunity to exchange information or opinions.

Business discussions with clients are frequently held over *ocha* in a coffee shop.

Ocha wo nomu

お茶を飲む

　日本人は，勤務時間中によくお茶を飲む。直訳すると，drink（飲む）tea（お茶）であるが，コーヒーを飲んでも，「お茶を飲む」といえる。

　勤め人が，朝オフィスにつく。まず第一にお茶を飲む。あと，10時すぎと午後3時ごろにもお茶が出る。来客でお茶，会議でもお茶だ。

　よく同僚を誘って，勤務時間中に会社を抜け出しては近くの喫茶店へ行ってお茶を飲む。目的は大体おしゃべりをすることだ。そこで，同僚に「お茶を飲みませんか」（How about a cup of tea?）と聞かれたら，ああ，あの人は，ふたりだけでおしゃべりしたくて誘っているのだな，と察する。このようなときのおしゃべりは，ふつう人事のうわさである。しばしば，お茶を飲むのは，情報交換の大切な場となっている。

　お客と商売の話をするときも，喫茶店で「お茶を飲みながら」ということがよくある。

CHOTTO IPPAI

On the surface of it, *chotto ippai* means 'let's have a quick drink'. It is one of the most frequently heard expressions among company staff members at the end of the day, but it does not mean that they are alcohol addicts. Sitting down together for a drink after work, before going home to dinner, gives salaried workers a chance to exchange information and talk about the day's work.

The boss suggests *chotto ippai* to a subordinate when he wants to admonish him privately or to hear his suggestions and complaints. In a way, it is an informal extension of communication on company and personnel matters. *Chotto ippai* is a practice that lubricates human relationships among company men.

An inexpensive drinking place is usually chosen for *chotto ippai*, partly because the boss pays for the drinks out of his own pocket.

ちょっと一杯

　直訳すると,「ちょっと一杯」は, "Let's have a quick drink." の意味であるが, 1日の仕事がひけたとき, 職場仲間で一番よく耳にすることばでもある。"のんべえ" だからではない。仕事が終わり, 家に帰って夕食をとるまえに, 仲間と一緒に飲めば, 情報の交換やら, 不平不満をぶつけることができる。ボスが部下に内々で注意したいときとか, 部下の意見や苦情を聞いてみようと思うとき,「ちょっと一杯」と誘う。いいかえれば, 非公式な仕事の延長でもある。

　ちょっと一杯をやるところは, たいていは安上がりの飲み屋である。こんなわけで,「ちょっと一杯」は, サラリーマンの人間関係に潤滑油の役を果たすものとでもいえようか。

AKA-CHŌCHIN

An *aka-chōchin* is a common venue for *chotto ippai*. *Aka* means 'red' and *chōchin*, 'lantern', but the phrase does not have the same connotations as 'red-light district' in English.

The *aka-chōchin* is a huge lantern about a metre in diameter made of paper over bamboo strips, and is prominently hung in front of drinking places to indicate that the shop serves sake and simple popular dishes. These places are cheap and have an informal friendly atmosphere. One can enjoy oneself for a couple of hours for less than US$10. The *aka-chōchin* is a sort of Japanese counterpart of the English pub.

In addition to the red lantern, a *nawa-noren* hangs at the door. This is a rope curtain, and *nawa-noren* is sometimes also used instead of *aka-chōchin* in referring to a bar.

See NOREN

赤ちょうちん

　日本のサラリーマンは，1日の仕事を終えて家路につく前に，「赤ちょうちん」へよく寄る。「赤」は red,「ちょうちん」は lantern だが，早とちりして red light（赤線区域）のことだ，などと思ってはいけない。

　この大ちょうちんは，竹ひごの骨組みに紙を貼った，直径1メートルほどのもの。日本式の一杯のみ屋の入口に，それとはっきり分かるようにぶらさげてある。「赤ちょうちん」は，「この店では，酒とちょっとしたおつまみ程度のものをお出しします。お値段は安く，気楽な仲間同士の雰囲気で楽しめます」という目印である。2時間ほど時を過ごしても，1人あたり10ドルとかからない。赤ちょうちんは，イギリスのパブの日本版と思えばいい。

　赤ちょうちんのほかに，入口にはしゅろで編んだなわで作った短いカーテン「縄のれん」がかかっている。「縄のれん」と「赤ちょうちん」はともに大衆酒場の意味につかわれる。

　→のれん

KANGEI-KAI and SŌBETSU-KAI

Kangei-kai is a welcoming party; and *sōbetsu-kai* is a sending off or farewell party. The Japanese hold such parties frequently. In the corporate world it is one of the ways in which staff are brought together. It also exemplifies the Japanese group culture.

When new staff join a company, a *kangei-kai* is held to welcome them. When someone is assigned to a new department, he is welcomed with a *kangei-kai*. When a member of the staff returns from an overseas posting, he is also given a *kangei-kai* welcome. Sake flows freely at the *kangei-kai* and the atmosphere is as relaxed as a Japanese corporate party can possibly be. The *kangei-kai* plays a very important role in Japanese society because it helps establish a feeling of belonging in the newcomer, or restores group identity in the man who has returned from abroad.

The *sōbetsu-kai* often turns out to be quite emotional. If the replacement is around at the time of the *sōbetsu-kai* (the farewell party), it may be combined with the *kangei-kai*. The party is then called a *kansōgei-kai*.

See OHAKO

歓迎会と送別会

　ビジネスマンも他の職業の人も，よく「歓迎会」(welcoming party) を開く。日本人の集団主義のあらわれのひとつである。新人が入社すると歓迎会を開く。新しい部課に配属されると歓迎会で迎えられる。海外勤務から帰任したときも歓迎会がある。歓迎会では酒が汲み交わされ，雰囲気がぐっと砕ける。歓迎会は日本の社会でとても重要な役割を果たす。新人または帰国者の所属意識を深め，集団精神を高め，団結を強め，一体感を密にする。

　歓迎会の逆が「送別会」(farewell or send-off party) である。出てゆく人のポストに代わりの人が新たにくるときは，歓迎会と送別会をひとまとめにして「歓送迎会」をするのがふつうである。

Bōnen-kai and shin-nen-kai

BŌNEN-KAI and SHIN-NEN-KAI

For the Japanese businessman, December is the month of the *bōnen-kai* office party. As the characters of the Chinese ideogram indicate, it is a 'forget-the-last-year party'.

Each section of a large company holds its own *bōnen-kai*, with every member of the staff chipping in to cover the cost. Because the year-end party is universal, tables in restaurants have to be reserved well in advance.

Alcohol flows fast and freely and breaks down inhibitions; disappointments, failures, frustrations and irritations of the receding year are washed away and successes are enthusiastically toasted.

With the past thus happily buried, or rather pickled in alcohol, everyone is ready to make a fresh start in the new year. Sometimes New Year parties are also held (*shin-nen-kai*), but usually there is only one or the other.

Bōnen-kai and shin-nen-kai

忘年会と新年会

　日本のサラリーマンにとって12月は,「忘年会」という宴会の月である。Forget-year-party, 読んで字のごとく, 1年の締めくくりになる。大会社では, 部課ごとに忘年会をやる。部課員はそれぞれに会費を出しあう。どこもかしこも年末パーティをやるので, かなり以前からレストランの席は予約しておかなければならない。

　酒がたくさんでる。この1年間の失敗やら不満, 落胆, 苛立ちを, 去りゆく時とともに洗い流してしまうには, 酒しかあるまい。もちろん, 良かったこと楽しかったことは, 思い出しては乾杯する。過去を水に流したり, アルコール漬けにして, さて気分一新, 新しい年の出発を迎えるのである。New-Year-party（新年会）をやるところもあるが, 大体忘年会をやったら新年会をやらないというように, どちらか一方をやるのがふつうである。

Bureikō

BUREIKŌ

Bureikō originally meant the meeting of people who were on intimate terms with each other, regardless of rank. Nowadays this word is heard at New Year parties (*shin-nen-kai*) and year-end parties (*bōnen-kai*) and at company excursions (*shain-ryokō*) in the form 'Let's go *bureikō* today.' This means: 'Let's forget about rank and seniority today and have a good time together as equals and friends.' In other words, it suggests that the rules of formality will be allowed to lapse for that time. The three individual words that make up the phrase help to define the meaning encompassed by *bureikō*. They are 'lack' or 'absence'; 'respect'; 'structure' or 'form'. A freer translation would be 'Rudeness is acceptable.'

In spite of the *bureikō* atmosphere of these gatherings, people will be addressed by their designations, or organisation titles such as *buchō* or *jomū* instead of . . . *-san*.

See -SAN

無礼講

　上下の別なく親しみあう仲間の集まりが元の意味だが,新年会,忘年会,あるいは社内旅行の宴会などで,席上「今日は無礼講でいこう」などという。社内の序列・役職の上下の別なく飲もう,楽しもう,との意味につかわれる。席上で多少失礼なことがあっても,大目に見ようということである。しかし,無礼講ではあっても,役職者には「部長」とか「常務」と職名で呼びかけ,単に「——さん」と呼びかけることはあまりない。

→ ——さん

OHAKO

Ohako is an art or skill in which one excels; in other words, one's forte or speciality. The reference is to something specific rather than general. For instance, one's *ohako* would not be 'playing golf' but the specific 'putting'. Some golfer's *ohako* may be to hit a bunker every time. At a party, participants are often called upon to perform their *ohako*, which may be a song, a card trick, or a juggling act.

The Chinese character for *ohako* can also be read *jūhachiban*, meaning No. 18. The original expression, which is still used today, is *kabuki jūhachiban*, meaning the 18 best plays in the repertoire of the Ichikawa family of kabuki actors. How did the characters for 18 come to be read *ohako*, which is literally 'honourable box'? One theory is that the Ichikawa family carefully kept the manuals on how to act the 18 plays in a box (*hako*).

At a *kangei-kai* or a *bōnen-kai* almost everyone is called upon to perform their *ohako*.

The word *kakushi-gei* (hidden talent) can be used in place of *ohako*.

おはこ（十八番）

「おはこ」は，秀でた芸なり技能をいう。いいかえれば，得手とか特殊技能である。全体的なことでなく，そのなかの特殊なことを指す。たとえば，ある人のおはこというとき，「ゴルフをやる」という全体のことではなく，なかでも「パット」がうまい，といった特定の技を指す。バンカーへかならず球を打ち込むのがおはこのゴルファーもいる。宴席でも，参加者におはこをやって，とせがむ。歌あり，手品あり，お座敷芸ありだ。

「おはこ」を漢字で書くと「十八番」(No. 18) である。もとは「歌舞伎十八番」で，いまもある演題である。もともとは，歌舞伎俳優の市川家に伝わるお家芸の18の狂言を指した。十八番と書いて，どうしておはこ（honorable box）と読むのだろう。一説には，市川家では，この十八の出し物の演じ方を秘伝として大切に箱（box）にしまっておいたからだという。

Shuntō

SHUNTŌ

The Japanese labour scene is a relatively calm and organised one compared to the battlefields of labour and management in the West. But the calm is not always there. The universal struggle goes on in Japan as it does all over the world, but with more restraint and order.

A major event in the industrial scene is the annual *shuntō*: the spring (*shun*) fight (*tō*) for wage increases.

Sohyo, one of the two largest labour federations in Japan (the other is Domei) carried out the first *shuntō* in 1955. In the initial years, only a few unions took part but gradually more and more joined until the *shuntō* became the biggest annual event in labour-management relations.

The *shuntō* formula was Sohyo's brainchild. Japanese labour unions, normally organised on a company basis and therefore not as effective, were brought together in this manner to present a united front. It moved wage negotiations from isolated company talks to industry-wide arenas, even though the unions were not organised on an industry basis.

Wage increases do not seem to trigger off price increases in Japan. There appears to be a tacit understanding between unions and management that the rates of wage increases must be kept in line with productivity increases.

春 闘

　日本では，労働組合のベースアップをはじめ各種の労働条件の改定闘争を，春の3～5月頃集中的に行なうところから，この名がついた。正確には春季労働闘争というべきだろう。

　総評（同盟と並ぶ日本最大の労働組合連合組織）がこの春闘を採用したのは1955年のことで，最初は少数の組合が参加したにすぎなかったが，その後参加組合が飛躍的に増大するとともに，すっかり定着し，いまやわが国労使関係における最大のイベントとなった。企業別組合という，わが国の労働組合の組織形態の弱さを克服する意図で，このような闘争方式が生まれた。ただ生産性向上率の枠内でのベースアップ率という労使暗黙の協調体制はあり，ベースアップが直ちに物価上昇の引き金にはなっていないようだ。

Lifetime employment

The Japanese personnel management system has been upheld as an ideal by many, and indeed it is a system that gets the optimum out of people. Although it is true that the whole system is peculiar to Japan, there are many elements that other industrial countries can adopt. But this sums up the aggregate: the individuals which every society throws up still struggle with the problem of fitting into standard patterns. Some of these problems are reflected in the words and phrases that follow.

MADOGIWA-ZOKU

Madogiwa is 'beside the window', and *zoku* is 'tribe'. In almost every big Japanese business corporation you will find the 'people by the window'. They are from the middle echelon of the management strata who may hold the title of 'manager' or 'sub-manager' but have no definite responsibilities or duties.

Although they may have played an active part in the company's business in their younger days, their climb up the promotional ladder had come to a standstill. Under the seniority system, in order to make way for the younger people, they have been pushed to the side and taken out of the mainstream of the business. With the lifetime employment system, they cannot be dismissed. But their rank is still respected and upheld and they are given the best desks in the general office – beside the window – where they sit waiting for their time to retire. The predicament of the *madogiwa-zoku* arose from the rigidity of the system.

窓際族

「窓際」とは beside the window,「族」は tribe である。日本では、大きな会社になると、まずどこにでも"window-side tribe" がいる。中間管理職クラスで、ふつうは部長とか次長の肩書をもっていながら、実際にやる仕事のない人達をいう。

若いころは、会社のために一所懸命尽くしたのに、昇進への階段をぱったり閉ざされてしまった人達である。年功序列制の下で、後進に道を譲るために現役の仕事をはずされる。しかし、終身雇用制なので、解雇するわけにはいかない。その格付けからいっても、オフィスの一番よい上席——窓際に机を与えられ、ここで定年を待つ。だから、「窓際族」は、うら哀しい響きがあることばである。

Teinen

TEINEN

The Japanese lifetime employment system does not really guarantee lifelong employment. Employment terminates at 55, 57 or 60, depending on different company policies, whereas the average life expectancy of the Japanese male is in the mid-70s. When the employee reaches the compulsory retirement age (*teinen*), he automatically loses his job, regardless of his physical and mental condition or ability.

Until a decade or so ago, 55 was the generally accepted retiring age, but it has been rising gradually. While some firms have brought it up to 60, the majority are still working on the age limits of the past.

The retiring employee receives a lump sum and with the government pension programme, he can usually live fairly comfortably for the rest of his life.

See SHŪSHIN-KOYŌ

定年

日本は終身雇用制だというが、厳密には、一生涯雇用を保証するわけではない。日本人の男子平均寿命は70歳代半ばとなったのに、雇用は、各会社の雇用規定により、55歳とか57歳、60歳で打ち切られる。従業員が「定年」(the age for compulsory retirement)に達すると、心身状態や能力にかかわりなく、自動的に職を失う。

10年くらい前は55歳がふつうの定年年齢だったが、いまは会社側が徐々に引き上げている。だが、年輩者がふえてきたにもかかわらず、古い定年制度を守っている会社も多い。

定年退職者は、一時金で退職手当を支給される。それと国から支給される年金があれば、老後のお金をそれほど心配せずに、どうにかやってゆける。

→終身雇用

Kata-tataki

KATA-TATAKI

Kata-tataki is a word dreaded by government servants who are past the age of 55. The term means 'tap on the shoulder', but in the civil service it has an ominous ring. A worker is approached gently by his superior with a hint that it's about time he thought of retiring from the service.

In the civil service, there is no fixed compulsory retirement age. Unless a worker retires of his own free will, the government cannot sack him. There are many men who stay on past 60 and even 70. Thus, the *kata-tataki* approach is used when the department head feels that the usefulness of an employee has ended. Against the background of the clear-cut private sector retirement system, this very singular method of deciding when a man has to go appears harsh and subjective; and whatever the merits of being able to use an experienced man to the limits of his efficacy, the old men in the organisation live in dread of the *kata-tataki*.

See KIBŌ-TAISHOKU

肩たたき

「肩たたき」と聞くと、55歳を過ぎた官公庁の職員は、ぞっとする。英語では、"tap on the shoulder"というだけのことだが、実は、公務員の間では不吉な響きをもつ。上役がやさしい物腰で近付いてくる——実際に肩をたたくことはないかもしれないが、もうそろそろ勇退してもいい頃合いではないか、といわんばかりに、やんわりとくる。公務員に定年はない。自由意思で辞めないかぎり、官庁側は解雇するわけにはいかない。だから、70歳を過ぎても、まだ頑張っているケースがある。そこで、官庁側が、あの人も歳のせいでもう役に立たなくなった、と判断したときに、肩たたき方式がとられる。首をタテに振らない人もなかにはいるが、大体は察しをつけて辞める。その方が、1号俸上がり、したがって退職金と年金がそれだけふえるからだ。

→ 希望退職

JIHYŌ

With the lifetime employment system, resignation is regarded as an extremely grave matter. If anyone wants to leave a company, he must submit a *jihyō*, a formal letter of resignation. An intent to resign transmitted verbally has no force and is completely ignored.

Quite often the management refuses to accept a *jihyō*, although it has no legal power to prevent an employee from leaving. However, in the Japanese social climate which demands a harmonious solution to everything it is socially difficult for anyone to leave his job unless the management agrees to let him go. If agreement is obtained, it becomes *en-man-taisha* – leaving a company in an amicable manner.

See KIBŌ-TAISHOKU, KATA-TATAKI

辞表

　日本は終身雇用制である。だから、一般に会社員が自分から辞めることはない。辞職はよほどの重大事、というのが通念になっている。会社を辞めたいときは、「辞表」（a formal letter of resignation）を提出せねばならない。口頭で辞意を伝えても効力はないし、まったく無視されてしまう。

　会社側が辞表を受理しないこともよくある。従業員がやめるのを阻止する権限などなにもないのに、である。しかし、日本の社会風土では、万事まるく納めるのがしきたりだから、会社側の同意がないのに辞めるのは、辞めた本人にとって不利となる。承諾があれば「円満退社」（leaving a company in an amicable manner）ということになる。

The Japanese character

The final section of this book explains words and expressions that are indicators of the Japanese character. The use of the word 'skin', for example, is quite different from many Western usages of 'skin'. We take the reader through a selected range, starting with the lowly stomach, the seat of many basic feelings, and ending with the word of utter finality, *kamikaze*, the winds of death.

Hara

HARA

Hara means 'stomach' or 'abdomen'. In the Japanese language it is the seat of emotions as much as the heart is. But it is only used for male emotions. Somehow the Japanese woman is not allowed to have the fire-in-the-belly feelings that a man has, and confines her emotions more delicately to the heart.

Hara occurs in a large number of phrases. *Hara-gei* is one. This is 'stomach art'. It describes a certain kind of technique: a technique of solving problems through negotiations without referring directly to the subject. In employing *hara-gei*, you do not reveal to the other party what is in your *hara*, but unmistakably and effectively convey to him your purpose, desire, demand, objective or advice. A whole book has been written about *hara-gei*.

Some other uses of *hara* in common phrases are given below:

Hara wo watte hanasu. 'to cut open the stomach': to have a heart-to-heart talk.

Hara wo miseru. 'to show the stomach': to reveal what is on one's mind.

Hara wo kukuru. 'to bundle up the stomach': to become resigned to something or resolve to do something whatever the outcome. (Note that both these meanings involve stifling one's feelings.)

腹

解剖学上からいうと「腹」はabdomen または stomach。これを比喩的につかうと,男性の心とか考えの意味になる。女性にはつかわない。腹に関しいろいろな言いまわしがある。

「腹芸」(stomach art)を主題に1冊の本を著した人にいわせれば,この日本式問題解決法をわずか数行で説明するなどは,おこがましいことであろう。「腹芸」とは,2人の間の交渉で,直接,ことばに出さずに問題を解決してしまう技術とでもいったらよい。腹の内にあるものを相手に明かさなくとも,目的なり,願望,要求,意図,忠告など,間違いなく,効果的にコミュニケートするのが腹芸である。そのためには,心理,直観,相手の個性,背景,狙い,個人的なつながり,それに相手がこちらをどの程度知っているか,といったいろいろの要素が必要だ。経験豊かで,冷静な神経の持ち主にして初めてうまくできることである。高い地位にある日本人同士のコミュニケーションは腹芸によることが多い。(→以心伝心)

「腹を割って話す」(to cut open the stomach and talk) = to have a heart-to-heart talk

「腹をみせる」(to show the stomach) = to reveal what is in one's mind

「腹をくくる」(to bundle up the stomach) = become resigned to or to resolve to (あきらめる,決心する)

Hara

Hara-guroi. 'the stomach is black': a treacherous person, a schemer.

Seppuku. 'to cut open the stomach'.

Puku is another way of reading the character for *hara*. Whenever the Japanese use a Chinese character, they have more than one sound, or more than one way of reading it. The first part of the word *seppuku* means 'cut'. So *seppuku* means 'cutting the stomach'. This is the proper word for the act which the world outside Japan knows as *hara-kiri*. *Seppuku* was the honourable course given to the feudal warrior in place of execution. The purpose of this act is to show that one's *hara* is clean.

Tsume-bara wo kiru – this also means *seppuku* or *hara-kiri*, but with specific reference to an instance when one does not want to commit *seppuku*. When people around you conspire and force you into a position in which you cannot help but carry out *seppuku*, this is known as *tsume-bara wo kiru*. The *tsume* prefix gives a sense of being crammed, or being boxed into a situation. The expression is used more loosely these days, and can be applied for instance to a circumstance where a person is forced by the people around him into a position where he has no recourse but to resign from his post or organisation.

「腹黒い」(stomach is black) = a treacherous person, a schemer（策士）

「切腹」（腹を切る）は，外国で"はらきり"といわれている行為の正式名称である。切腹とは，封建時代に，処刑に代わり武士に与えられた名誉ある刑であった。これは，切腹するものが，自分の腹はきれいなんだということを証明するための行為であった。（→懐刀）

「詰め腹を切る」は，意志に反して，無理に腹を切らされることをいう。廻りの者たちが，ある人物を切腹せざるをえないような状況に追いこんだとき，その人物に「詰め腹を切らせる」という。今日では，周囲の人達がよってたかって，無理に辞任を強いるときに，この言葉がつかわれる。

「自腹を切る」(to cut one's own stomach) とは，自分の小遣いから支払うことをいう。

Hara-no-mushi

HARA-NO-MUSHI

There are a whole set of phrases that seem to suggest that the Japanese have all sorts of worms in their stomachs. *Mushi* means 'worm', and *hara-no-mushi* is 'worm in the stomach', or 'the stomach's worm'. One of these worms has the gift of prescience and tells a person that he will be promoted or sent on an assignment abroad or lose a contract, etc. This is *mushi ga shiraseru*, and is like a sixth sense about the future. When one is in a bad mood for no particular reason, the worm in the stomach is not in its proper place – *mushi no idokoro ga warui* (the worm is not settled properly).

If one takes a dislike to a person for no apparent reason, it is because *mushi ga sukanai* (the worm does not like him or her). When one suffers a loss and cannot get over it, his *hara-no-mushi ga osamaranai* (the worm in the stomach is not calmed down). When a baby has a severe stomach ache, it is because *kan no mushi* (the worm in its spleen) is acting violently. *Kan* is spleen, or entrails generally, and in this context is equivalent to stomach.

See KI

腹の虫

　正編で述べたように腹は多様な働きをもつが、この腹のなかにはある種の虫が棲んでいて、宿主の感情を支配する。はっきりした理由もないのに嫌いな人間は「虫が好かない」からであり、不利益をこうむってなすすべもないときには「腹の虫がおさまらない」。近い将来起こることを漠然と予感するのは「虫が知らせる」からであり、なんとなく不機嫌なのは「虫の居どころが悪い」(虫が危険な場所にいる) からである。幼児がひきつけや激しい腹痛を起こすのも「疳 (かん) の虫」が暴れるからである。

　近年まで日本人は、寄生虫の罹病率が高く、胃や腸のなかに寄生する寄生虫が実際に種々の症状や苦痛を引き起こしていたので、この事実からの連想で上記のような言葉が生まれたものらしい。現在、寄生虫はほとんど駆除されてしまったが、言葉のうえの「腹の虫」は、社会生活におけるストレスの増大のためか、相変わらず健在である。

　→気

Hada

HADA

Hada is 'skin', but apart from its basic meaning, it is used to denote temperament, character, disposition, bent, type, mould, etc. It is a very personal word.

Hada-zawari means 'feel' or 'touch', as in a soft or rough touch. In reference to a person, we say *hada-zawari ga yawarakai* (His touch is soft). This means that he is gentle-mannered, affable, courteous.

Hada ni awanai is 'not agreeable to the skin'. It is a polite way of saying that one does not like a certain person. It is also used for two people who cannot get used to each other or who are not compatible with each other. If someone feels uncomfortable in his job, he can also say that it is a *hada ni awanai* position for him. The opposite is *hada ni au*. 'It fits my style', or 'It goes with my skin, my personality.'

Hada is used to sum up a man's personality. A scholarly type would be called *gakusha-hada: gakusha* means 'an academic'. Thus a politically inclined person would be known as a *seijika-hada*; a scientific type, a *kagakusha-hada*; a diplomat, a *gaikōkan-hada*; an arty person, a *geijutsuka-hada*, etc.

肌

「肌」は skin。比喩に使うと, temperament（気質）, character（性格）, disposition（性癖）, bent（好み）, type（型）, mold（たち）といった意味である。かならずしも, 品の悪い意味ではない。

「肌ざわり」といえば, feel（感触）とか touch（触覚）。肌にふれた感じが硬いとかやわらかいこと。人にいうときには,「肌ざわりがやわらかい」（soft）という。gentle-mannered（物腰のおだやかな）, affable（丁寧な）, courteous（丁重な）人をいう。

「肌に合わない」とは, not suitable or agreeable to the skin（なんとなく, 気持ちが合わない）こと。あの人は好きじゃない, ということの遠回しないい方。また, 二人が互いにぴったりしないこと, 性格や物の考え方, 好み, 興味などの違いから, 一緒にやってゆけないことも「肌に合わない」である。あるポストが自分の性分に合わなくて, いやだいやだと思っているばあい, そのポストは,「肌に合わない」のである。勝手が違って本領が発揮できない（a fish out of water）と思っている意味。その反対は「肌に合う」である。（→気に入る）

あの人は学者タイプ（scholarly type）だとか, 学問に向いている（academic bent）といいたければ, 肌がつかわれる。たとえば,「学者肌」だというように。学者を別の言葉におきかえてもよい。「政治家肌」「商人肌」「科学者肌」「外交官肌」「芸術家肌」など。

Shita, kuchi

SHITA, KUCHI

Kuchi, the mouth, and *shita*, the tongue, are two words that have uncomplimentary undertones. Perhaps it is because the Japanese do not believe in being outspoken, nor in showing their feelings indiscriminately to strangers, and the mouth and tongue are the instruments of rudeness and indiscretions.

Nimai-jita, a forked tongue, has the same meaning as the English expression for the person who is a double-dealer.

Kuchi-guruma ni noseru (loosely, to take a person for a ride on one's mouth-wheel) is to fool someone with sweet talk.

Kōzetsu no to, where *kō* is an alternative phonetic reading of the mouth character, and *zetsu* for tongue, is a person who stirs up controversy through careless talk.

Shitasaki-sanzun (tip of the tongue three inches) describes a person with a smooth tongue who tries to glibly explain away his failures and mistakes.

One complimentary expression with the word 'mouth' in it is *kuchi hattchō te hattchō* (skilful with the mouth, dexterous with the hands). This refers to the man who is not only articulate but who also gets things done.

If you do something sensational, you astonish people and make them 'roll up their tongues': *shita wo maku*.

A modern term which is a good example of the ingenious way in which the Japanese adapt and assimilate foreign words, is *kuchi-komi*. *Komi* is a dis-

Shita, kuchi

舌，口

どういうわけか、「舌」(tongue)と「口」(mouth)に関係ある日本語の表現には、あまり褒めたことばでないものが多い。たとえば、あの人は「二枚舌」(double-tongue)をつかうという。裏表があったり、嘘をつくので、いうことに信用がおけないことを指す。

「口車に乗せる」(しいて訳せば take a person on a ride on one's mouth wheel) とは、甘言で釣ること (to take a person in with sweet talk) である。

「口舌の徒」(kō は mouth, zetsu は tongue の音読み) といえば、口先がうまく、禍を起こす人。

「舌先三寸」(tip of the tongue three inches) とは、ことばたくみにしゃべること、自分の間違いや失敗をいいくるめて、ごまかしてしまうこと。

口をつかった婉曲な表現には「口八丁、手八丁」(skilful with the mouth, skilful with the hand) がある。弁舌さわやかで、しかも、やることもきちんとしている人のこと。

なにかすぐれたことをした人には「舌を巻く」(roll up the tongue)。つまり感嘆する (astonish)。

外国語を採り入れて同化してしまうのは、日本人のお家芸だ。新感覚の表現には、これが多い。その一例に「口コ

215

tortion of the English word 'communication'. The phrase means 'communication by word of mouth'. This is one of many bastardised words used today in which the first half is a Japanese word, the other being a very distorted English word.

See KARA-OKE

KOSHI

As a pivot of the body, *koshi*, the hips, waist, loin, is used in many phrases to describe ways of doing things, and the poise and style of a man.

For example, *koshi ga hikui* (low hips) is modest, humble, polite, unassuming, and conversely *koshi ga takai* (high hips) is proud, haughty, 'riding the high horse'.

A person who is *koshi ga karui* (light) is one who is quick to act, nimble or willing to work. It has recently also taken on the meaning of 'fleet-footed' for a job-hopper. A woman who is *koshi ga karui* is similarly one who flits from man to man. Conversely a person whose waist is *omoi* (heavy) is one who dilly-dallies and is unwilling or slow at work.

Koshi wo ageru is to raise the waist, which not only means to physically get up from a sitting position, but also describes a person who has been watching a situation and has now decided to move in and take action.

ミ」がある。「コミ」は英語の communication の変造。これに日本語の「口」を組み合わせて mouth communication つまり by word of mouth である。

腰

「腰」(waist, hip, loin) は身体の大事な部分なので、これをつかった表現は多い。たとえば、「腰が低い」(low) とか「高い」(high) という。低いのは humble (謙遜)、modest (穏やか)、unassuming (高ぶらない)、polite (丁寧な) こと。反対に「腰が高い」のは proud (高慢) とか haughty (横柄) なこと。

「腰が軽い」(light) といえば、"quik to act"（気軽に動き出す）、nimble（すばしこい）、または "willing to work"（積極的にやる）人のこと。逆に、「腰が重い」(heavy) とは、"slow to act"（なかなか動き出さない）、"unwilling to work"（あまりやる気がない）、または dilly-dallies（ぐずぐずする）人のこと。腰が軽いを女性には使わぬ方がよろしい。男の誘いに簡単に乗る尻軽女にとられるからだ。

「腰を上げる」は "to raise the waist"。座っている場所から立ち上がることだが、情勢を観望したのちに、やっと行動に移る決心を固めることにもいう。(→ みこし)

Ki

Koshi wo sueru is to let the waist settle down, which means to settle down to a steady course of action or to undertake something seriously or with determination.

To do something with *oyobi-goshi* is to do it in an unsteady stance, with a bent back, or leaning over. Thus, it describes a person whose heart is not in his work.

Koshi-kudake is a person whose waist breaks down, in other words a weak-kneed person. This term comes from the Japanese wrestling sport of sumo and is applicable to a contestant who breaks down in the middle of a wrestling match. It is used for someone who cracks up at a crucial moment, say, during business negotiations.

When an event causes 'one's hip to become disjointed' (*koshi ga nukeru*), he is overwhelmed by the enormity of the thing or paralysed with fear.

KI

Ki is an abstract concept that covers the spirit, mind, heart, will, intention, feelings, mood, nature and disposition. It is the essence of a thing. It can also mean care, precaution, attention, concern, air, atmosphere, flavour, and smell. Expressions given here are those which relate to the first group of abstract meanings of the spirit.

A very popular expression is *ki wa kokoro* (*ki* is the heart), which means the gesture may be small but it shows sincerity or goodwill or genuine gratitude.

「腰を据える」は "to let the waist settle down"。じっくりと着実に行動すること。真剣に，決意を固めて事に取り組むことをいう。

「及び腰で事をする」とは，腰をまげたり(bent back)，前かがみ (leaning over)の不安定な姿勢で動作すること (to do it in an unsteady position)。本気で取り組む気持ちにない人を指す。

「腰くだけ」は "a person whose waist breaks down" とか "a weak-kneed person" (弱腰の人)。相撲からきたことばで，取り組みの最中に，受けこたえる腰の力がなくなって転がること。ここから商取引の大事な局面で，あとが続かずに潰れてしまうことをいう。

なにかの出来事で「腰が抜ける」(hip to become disjointed)とは，その物すごさに圧倒されて動けなくなること，恐怖でへなへなになってしまうこと。

気

「気」はいろいろにつかわれる。権威ある辞典によると，spirit（精神），mind（心），heart（気持ち），will（決意），intention（意思），feeling（感情），mood（気分），nature（性質），disposition（性癖），care（注意），precaution（用心），flavor（香），smell（匂），とある。つかい方で意味も違ってくる。

一番よく使われるのが「気は心」("Ki is heart.")。意味は，形にあらわれたものがささやかであっても，内に誠

Ki

If you feel *ki ni kuwanai* about the performance of your subordinate, he should get worried because it means that you are not happy with his output or attitude. If you feel that your boss is a *ki ni kuwanai* person, it means you think he is a disagreeable fellow. This is somewhat similar to *hada ni awanai*, but it is directed more at the basic nature of the man than saying that you and he are incompatible. The opposite is *ki ni iru*: to like, to fit in, to suit.

When someone pulls out the *ki* (*ki wo nuku*), it means that he has lost interest, or is discouraged. The spirit has been drawn out of him and his soul has been emptied. When *ki* 'does not go into' any endeavour or project (*ki ga hairanu*) it evokes no interest. *Ki* is 'not going in'. *Nu* is a negative suffix.

Ki can also be massaged, rubbed, manipulated: *ki wo momu* means a person worried about something, and who is nervous and fidgety. *Ki wo momaseru* (one's *ki* is massaged) means 'to keep a person in suspense'. His *ki* is being rubbed down.

Ki wo hiku (to draw out the *ki*) is to sound out the intentions of the other party.

Kinori usu (the *ki* is thin) means 'lacklustre', 'lethargy', 'stagnation'. It can be used to describe a dead stock market.

意とか心からの感謝，助けたい気持ちなどがこもっていること。部下の仕事振りが「気に食わない」とは，unsatisfactory（不満）だったり，displease（不機嫌）であること（「肌に合わない」参照）。この反対は「気に入る」to like, to find agreeable, to suit one's taste である。

「気を抜く」（pull out the ki）とは，unenthusiastic（身を入れない），lukewarm（気乗りしない），discouraged（意欲を失っている），dispirited（元気のない），careless（不注意な）こと。事をやるのに「気が入らぬ」（ki does not go into）とは，熱が入らない（cannot become enthusiastic）のこと。

Ki は，rub や massage することもできる——「気を揉む」である。このばあいは，なにかにくよくよ心配したり（worried, anxious），神経質になったり（nervous），落ちつかない（fidgety）こと。「気を揉ませる」は，人を suspense や tenterhook（宙ぶらりん）の状態におくこと。

「気を引く」は，相手の意向を探ること。

株の用語に「気乗り薄」（ki-ride-thin）がある。市況が lackluster（活気がない），lethargic（低調），stagnant（低迷）の意。

Te

TE

Being the part of the body which is most useful to man, *te*, the hand, figures in a great number of expressions.

Te wo tsukeru is to use your hand, as in diversifying and starting a new business.

Te wo utsu (*utsu* is to hit) is to strike a deal and to do the necessary things like getting a bank loan and recruiting staff to start a new business.

Te wo hiku is to withdraw your hand, to withdraw from a deal.

Te-ochi is a slip of the hand: an error, an oversight, a fault.

Te no uchi is the inside of the palm, associated therefore with one's real intentions. It is applied in the same way as the English phrase 'to show your hand'.

Te ni amaru describes a man who is uncompromising and unreasonable. He is holding on to too much in his hand.

O-te-age, as the English would say, is to throw up your hands in dismay. Or like the Italians?

Similarly, *te wo yaku* is to burn your hands, or to be in big trouble.

Te wo kiru, to cut off the hands, is to sever connections or to stop dealing with someone.

Te

手

　体のもっとも重要な部分である手（hand）をつかった表現は実にたくさんある。ここでは，ほんの数例をあげるにとどめる。

　事業をひろげるとか，新規に始めるとき，新しい商売（new business）に「手をつける」。その商売の資金手当てをするため，銀行に「手を打っ」て融資を求める。必要なことを確実にやれるように措置する意味につかう。たとえば売買交渉の決着をつけるのも「手を打つ」である。その支払いを「手形」（bill）で受け取るといったい方もある。「手を引く」は中止である。

　契約書を作るとき，「手落ち」（slip, careless error, oversight）がないかどうか確かめる。契約書に間違いがあれば，あなたの「手落ち」になる（your fault, your blame）。

　交渉では，自分の「手の内をみせる」（show your hand）まえに，相手の「手の内」（inside of the palm ＝ intentions）を探ろうとする。相手が頑固（obstinate）で，分からず屋（unreasonable）で，妥協しない（uncompromising）と，「手に余る」（too much for the hand ＝ intractable, unmanageable）。そこで，あきらめて「手をあげる」。すなわち，「お手上げ」（give up, at a loss what to do）となる。たいへんな困難や厄介事にぶつかって「手を焼く」（experiencing so much difficult or trouble）と，もう「手を切り」（cut the hand ＝ stop dealing with, cut off connections）たくなる。

Kara-oke

Te wo nuku is 'cutting corners', as in sacrificing quality in manufacturing. It implies a withdrawing of the hand. Akin to shutting one eye.

KARA-OKE

Kara is Japanese for 'empty' and *oke* is the first part of the corruption of the English 'orchestra'. The Japanese delight in creating words like this: part English, part Japanese. Examples are: *katsu-don*, meaning a bowl of rice topped with pork cutlet. *Katsu* is from cutlet; *donburi* is a bowl. *Jari-tare* means child entertainer: *jari* is child; *tare* is from *tarento*, talented. *Nama-kon* means ready-mix concrete: *nama* is raw, crude, half-done; and *kon* is from *konkurīto*, concrete.

Kara-oke is a cassette tape with only an orchestral accompaniment recorded on it. The singers' voices are not recorded. Bars and *aka-chōchin* everywhere have *kara-oke* for their customers who are slightly tipsy and feel that they should display their singing *ohako* (talent) to the accompaniment of a full orchestra. People who have never met each other before will join in the singing and clink each others' cups and glasses together and a great spirit of bonhomie and friendliness is created.

Kara-oke may be a nuisance to those who want to have a quiet drink, but to the keyed-up businessman, it is a great way to work off frustration and relax after a tiring day at work.

See AKA-CHŌCHIN, OHAKO

日本市場向けの製品を作るとき決して「手を抜い」てはならない。日本のお客は目がこえているからだ。「手を抜く」とは，cut corner の悪い意味で，手間を省いたり（economize on labor），きちんと気を配らなかったり，工程をとばすことをいう。

カラオケ

カラ（empty）と「オーケストラ」（orchestra）との合成語である。この種の合成語づくりは日本人の特技である。カツドン（katsu-retsu←cutlet＋domburi）＝ご飯の上に pork cutlet を載せた食物。半ズボン（han＝half＋zubon←jupon＝pants）＝short pants。ジャリタレ（jari＝child＋tarento←talent）＝子供の俳優・歌手。生コン（nama＝crude, half-done, rare＋konkuriito←concrete）＝ready mix cement。それこそ無数にある。

カラオケは，伴奏のオーケストラ曲をカセットテープで聞かせる装置。いたるところのバーや赤ちょうちんに置かれ，少々酒の入った客がカセットのオーケストラを従えて自慢の歌を披露する。見知らぬ客同士が歌い合い，酒を呑み，たちまちに意気投合することもある。静かに酒を呑みたい人はいささか迷惑だが，カラオケ・バーは，1日の仕事の疲れを癒やし，うさを晴らすのに最高の場所となっている。

→赤ちょうちん

Kamikaze

KAMIKAZE

Twice in the 13th century, 1274 and 1281, Mongolian forces attempted to invade Japan, but on both occasions the invading fleet was destroyed by a typhoon and Japan was saved. The people believed that the propitious typhoons were sent by God and they named them *kamikaze*: winds of the gods, or divine winds.

The Japanese are not a particularly religious people, but in times of distress they hope and pray for a *deus ex machina*, a *kamikaze* to come to their aid. During the last war they created the *kamikaze* themselves, in one sense, with the suicide corps of pilots who crash-dived their planes into enemy ships. Looking at it the other way, naming these pilots the *kamikaze* must have had tremendous psychological effect on them and on the whole nation, making them feel that they were indeed part of the divine plans of the gods.

Today the word is used in two ways. Hoping for a *kamikaze* to blow (*kamikaze ga fuku*), may be hoping for an exceptionally large order to come in and save a firm which is in financial distress. Taking the meaning from the war use of the word, a *kamikaze* can be used to describe a reckless taxi driver or a rash act that endangers one's life.

Kamikaze

神風が吹く

　鎌倉時代の1274年と1281年の2度にわたって蒙古の軍隊が来襲したが，その都度，偶然にも台風が吹き荒れ，蒙古の船は難破・沈没し，そのため日本は侵略を免れることができた。この日本にとって幸運な大風は神の加護によって吹いた風（＝神風），との信仰が生まれた。

　その例から，企業あるいは産業界では，それまでの独自の最善の努力にもかかわらず先行きの見通しがまったくたたず四苦八苦しているときに，ふだん信仰心の薄い日本人でも，苦しいときの神だのみ「神風が吹いてくれないかなあ」と思うことがある。一つの大きな出来事から，大量の製品の注文を受けて，爆発的に企業が成長することを期待して。

INDEX

Abura wo uru, 106
Ada, 120
Aisatsu-mawari, 118
Aka, 182
Aka-chōchin, 182, 224
Ama-kudari, 86
Aota-gai, 172, 174
Aota-gari, 174
Apointo, 108
Arigatō, 22
Arubaito, 152, 154
Banzai, 104
Batsu, 50, 52, 100
Bōnasu, 160, 162
Bōnen-kai, 186, 188, 190
Buchō, 34, 124, 188
Bureikō, 188
Chihō-batsu, 52
Chōchin, 182
Chōrei, 146, 177
Chotto, 40
Chotto ippai, 180, 182
Chotto matte, 42
Chotto matte kudasai, 42
Chūto-saiyō, 168
Dame-oshi, 102
Dōki, 172
Dōmo, 22
Dōsōsei, 54
En, 90
Endan, 90
En ga aru, 90
En·man-taisha, 202
En wo kiru, 90

Fudai, 70
Futokoro-gatana, 74
Gaijin, 28, 96, 98
Gaikōkan-hada, 212
Gaku-batsu, 50, 52
Gakusha, 212
Gakusha-hada, 212
Gashi-kōkan, 116
Geba, 94
Gebahyō, 94
Geijutsuka-hada, 212
Giri, 100
Giri ga karamu, 100
Giri-gatai hito, 100
Giri ippen, 100
Giri no naka, 100
Giri wo hatasu, 100
Go-en, 90
Gogatsu-byō, 172
Gokurō-sama, 40
Gomasuri, 66
Goshūgi, 114
Goshūgi-sōba, 114
Goshūgi-torihiki, 114
Ha-batsu, 50
Hada, 212
Hada ni au, 212
Hada ni awanai, 212, 220
Hada-zawari ga yawarakai, 212
Hai, 18
Hanko, 130, 136, 138
Hara, 206, 208
Hara-gei, 206

228

Index

Hara-guroi, 208
Hara-kiri, 74, 208
Hara-no-mushi, 210
Hara-no-mushi ga osamaranai, 210
Hara wo kukuru, 206
Hara wo miseru, 206
Hara wo watte hanasu, 206
Hijikake-isu, 76
Hiru-andon, 72
Hon·ne, 92
Ie, 18
Insei, 82
Irasshai-mase, 24
Ishin-denshin, 56
Jari-tare, 224
Jihyō, 202
Jiko-taishoku, 144
Jinji-idō, 150, 152
Jin-myaku, 46
Jirei, 150
Jō, 120
Jōmu, 188
Ka, 124
Kachō, 124, 126
Kagakusha-hada, 212
Kaigi, 126
Kakarichō, 126
Kaki-ire-doki, 112
Kaki-kyūka, 164, 166
Kakushi-gei, 190
Kamikaze, 226
Kamikaze ga fuku, 226
Kangei-kai, 184, 190

Kan no mushi, 210
Kansōgei-kai, 184
Kao, 42
Kao ga hiroi, 44
Kao ga kiku, 44
Kao wo kasu, 44
Kao wo tateru, 42
Kao wo tsubusu, 42
Kao wo tsunagu, 44
Kao wo uru, 44
Kara-oke, 224
Kasei, 124
Kata-tataki, 200
Katsu-don, 224
Kekkō desu, 36
Kei-batsu, 50
Keikōtō, 72
Ki, 218
Kibō-taishoku, 142, 144
Ki ga hairanu, 220
Ki ni iru, 220
Ki ni kuwanai, 22
Kinori usu, 220
Kiremono, 74
Ki wa kokoro, 218
Ki wo hiku, 220
Ki wo momaseru, 220
Ki wo momu, 220
Ki wo nuku, 220
Kogai, 70
Kōhai, 52, 54
Konjō, 68
Konjō ga aru, 68
Konjō ga nai, 68

Index

Koshi, 216
Koshi ga hikui, 216
Koshi ga karui, 216
Koshi ga nukeru, 216
Koshi ga takai, 216
Koshi-kudake, 216
Koshi wo ageru, 216
Koshi wo sueru, 218
Kōzetsu no to, 214
Kubi, 78
Kubi ga mawaranai, 78
Kubi ga tobu, 78
Kubi-kiri, 78
Kubi wo hineru, 78
Kubi wo kakete, 78
Kuchi, 214
Kuchi-guruma ni noseru, 214
Kuchi hattchō te hattchō, 214
Kuchi-komi, 214
Kugi wo sasu, 102
-kun, 34
Kuromaku, 80, 84
Madogiwa, 196
Madogiwa-zoku, 196
Magete, 134
Mai hōmu, 86
Mai-hōmu-shugisha, 86
Mawata de kubi wo shimeru, 78
Meishi, 138
Meishi-kōkan, 116
Mushi, 210
Mushi ga idokoro ga warui, 210
Mushi ga shiraseru, 210
Mushi ga sukanai, 210

Naishoku, 154
Nama-kon, 224
Nasake, 120
Nawa-noren, 182
Negai, 132
Nemawashi, 58, 128, 130
Newaza, 84
Newaza-shi, 84
Nimai-jita, 214
Nippachi, 110, 112
Noren, 94, 96
Noren-wake, 96
Ocha, 178
Ocha wo nomu, 178
Ochūgen, 100, 112
Ōgosho, 82
Ohako, 190, 224
Oil-shokku, 144
Okaeri-nasai, 26
Okagesamade, 28
Omoi, 216
On, 120
On-gaeshi, 120
On ni kiseru, 120
On-shirazu, 120
On wo ada de kaesu, 120
On wo uru, 120
Oseibo, 100, 112
O-te-age, 222
Otsukare-sama, 40
Oya no on, 120
Oyobi-goshi, 218
Ringi, 130
Ringi-sho, 130

Index

Rōnin, 64
–san, 34, 188
San·mon-ban, 136
Sayonara, 20, 32
Seifuku, 148
Seijika-hada, 212
Seiri-kyūka, 168
Senpai, 52, 54
Seppuku, 208
Shachō, 34
Shain-ryō, 164
Shain-ryokō, 188
Shaka, 148
Shakun, 146, 148
Sha-taku, 164
Shaze, 146, 148
Shimbun jirei, 150
Shin·nen-kai, 186, 188
Shin·nyu-shain, 172
Shita, 214
Shitasaki-sanzun, 214
Shita wo maku, 214
Shitsurei shimasu, 32
Shūgi, 114
Shukkō-shain, 156
Shuntō, 192
Shūshin-koyō, 142
Sōbetsu-kai, 184
Soko wo magete nantoka, 134
Soko wo nantoka, 134
Sumimasen, 22, 30, 32
Suri-awase, 58, 60
Tadaima, 26
Tadaima kaeri-mashita, 26
Tanshin-ryō, 164
Tatemae, 92
Te, 222
Teate, 158
Teiki-saiyō, 170
Teinen, 198
Tenbiki, 160
Te ni amaru, 222
Te no uchi, 222
Te-ochi, 222
Te wo hiku, 222
Te wo kiru, 222
Te wo nuku, 224
Te wo tsukeru, 222
Te wo utsu, 222
Te wo yaku, 222
Todoke, 132
Tomo-bataraki, 154
Tomo-kasegi, 154
Tozama, 70, 84, 86
Tsume-bara wo kiru, 208
Uogokoro areba mizugokoro, 60
Yakudoshi, 110
Yoroshiku, 20
Yūkyū-kyūka, 166, 168
Zaibatsu, 84
Zensho shimasu, 38
Zoku, 196

ABOUT THE EDITOR

Rex Shelley studied Chemistry at the University of Malaya in Singapore, and thereafter read Engineering and Economics at Gonville and Caius College, University of Cambridge, United Kingdom. It was during the war years that he was first exposed to the Japanese language, an interest which he later took up and has been pursuing actively for the last ten years.

In his dealings with Japanese engineering firms and general trading companies over the past fifteen years, he has had occasion to observe and learn from Japanese business management, apart from which it has also led to an awareness that miscommunication can arise due to an improper understanding of the delicate shades of meaning inherent in the Japanese language. An avid reader of contemporary Japanese fiction, Rex Shelley hopes that eventually many more Japanese novels will be translated into English, enabling them to be appreciated by more than the privileged few.